What People Are Saying about

Souls Under Siege...

In his book, Souls Under Siege, Pastor Vining offers to his readers a variety you might even say a smorgasbord. His menu consists of healthy "soul food" that will help us be prepared for the enemy's attack. We also find "preventive exercises" that can help us avoid the devil's attempt to destroy us. Yes, in this book there is something for everyone, there's food that will satisfy the spiritual appetite as it provides strength and growth for our daily Christian walk.

- David Lanier–

With insight and clarity, Pastor Don Vining explores critical issues concerning our freedom in Christ. In a world of increasing darkness believers who apply these biblical principles of victory will shine forth a powerful and attractive testimony of Christ's liberty.

- Dr. David Ferguson-
- Intimate Life Ministries –

ISBN 978-1-969865-29-9 (Paperback)
ISBN 978-1-969865-30-5 (Ebook)

Inquiries and Book Orders should be addressed to:
Leavitt Peak Press
17901 Pioneer Blvd Ste L #298, Artesia, California 90701
Phone #: 2092191548

Souls Under Siege

BY
PASTOR DON R. VINING

CONTENTS

DEDICATION

This book is dedicated to the ministry and many years of love and compassion that Lindsey and Lucille Croft shared in this life. I suppose that no one could talk about heaven the way Brother Lindsey Croft could. Our lives were truly strengthened and I know heaven is a brighter place since the arrival of these dear ones.

ACKNOWLEDGMENTS

A special love to my beautiful bride of Forty five years and my awesome daughters Sheena and Brittany without these three there would be an incredible void in my life and ministry.

My thanks to Connie Neumann, who only by God's anointing could have taken hundreds of pages of notes and captured my personality and message in this book.

My appreciation to Kay Dunn for her many hours of dedicated service to this project.

Also my gratitude to Suzi Scott for a great job in proof reading.

Thank you Dr. Rose Sims for your encouragement and insight in the distribution of this book project.

FOREWORD

By Dr. Rose Sims

If this remarkable book doesn't light your fire, then your wood is wet! Churches in America are in trouble. Once we were a church on fire. We realized we were in a spiritual warfare. Then we forgot about souls under siege.

Barna research indicates that today there is not a county in the United States that has a larger percentage of Christians than it had ten years ago. This is not a mere statistic; it is a matter of eternal life or eternal death.

Eighty percent of all church growth in complacent America is sim-ply transfer of membership. Hundreds of churches that call themselves evangelical list no professions of faith year after year. Even more tragically, countless souls who do come to the altar in a time of real emotional conviction are all too often soon lost to the church and are harder to win back than if they had never come to the altar.

Souls Under Siege is a thought provoking book which is a must for every pastor and lay person who truly is willing to get involved to a point of inconvenience, understands the difference between a decision and a real conversion and who is willing to do battle for the souls of mankind.

INTRODUCTION

As Christians, we must know that the devil is alive and well on planet Earth. I believe that Christians are the only restraining force for the final act of Satanic takeover. We, as believers, are called upon to do the greatest job that any church or believer has ever been called upon to do in history. We are called upon to shake this world and get it ready for the greatest event that the world shall ever know. Jesus Christ is coming back to earth again.

The Bible tells us that we are in an inward battle. Romans 7:22-23 says, "For I delight in the law of God after the inward man. But I see another law in my members, warring against the law of my mind, and bringing me into captivity to the law of sin which is in my members." We know that it's a spiritual battle. "For the weapons of our warfare are not carnal, but mighty before God to the pulling down of strongholds" (2 Cor. 10:4).

We must know that the God we serve is mightier than the battles that come against us. Ephesians 6:10 says, "For we wrestle not against flesh and blood, but against principalities, against powers, against the rulers of the darkness of this world, against spiritual wickedness in high places."

We also know that "Ye are of God, little children, and have overcome them: because greater is he that is in you than he that is in the world" (1 John 4:4).

As believers, we do not have time for church splits. We do not have time for power struggles. We do not have time to put down our brothers and sisters. We do not have time to be confused about what the enemy wants to do in our lives. We cannot afford to play carnal games. We've got to emulate the mind of Christ.

Satan would like us to have a reprobate mind (Rom. 1:28). He would like you to have a fuddled mind (Eph. 4:17). He would like you to have a puffed-up mind; a carnal mind; or a defiled mind (Col. 2:18; Rom. 8:7; Titus 1:7).

But God's call is very different. He wants us to have a spiritual mind (Rom. 8:6). In Romans 12:2, He calls us to have a transformed mind. He calls us to have a mind like Christ, a renewed mind, and a sound mind (1 Cor. 2:16, Eph. 4:23, 2 Tim. 1:7).

God also calls us to Philippians 4:8: "Finally, brethren, whatsoever things are true, whatsoever things are honest, whatsoever things are just, whatsoever things are pure, whatsoever things are lovely, whatsoever things are of good report: if there be any virtue, if there be any praise, think on these things."

The enemy will go to extremes to deceive you and tear down your faith. Understand that you can never be effective in serving the Lord and withstanding the attacks of Satan until you learn how he comes against believers.

Souls Under Siege will get into the heart of what the enemy wants to do in your life. It will also help you understand how you can endure and overcome the attacks on your life. As you read through these pages, I encourage you to ask the almighty God to give you wisdom, knowledge, and much understanding in how you can be an overcomer.

Remember, greater is he that is in you, than what is coming against you. It is my prayer that God will move you to a new level of understanding and power in your Christian walk.

For maximum results from this book, read it carefully and prayerfully a little at a time searching for the treasure of truth for your own need.

CHAPTER ONE

KNOW YOUR ENEMY

It is important to know your enemy. Often, believers are fine and happy until you mention the name of the devil. Then they get real quiet and fear comes over them. "Oh, you don't want to mess with the devil," they say.

If you're saved, you've already messed with the devil. You've already worked yourself against what he stands for. He wants to destroy your mind and your heart. He wants to destroy your family, and he wants to destroy your job. He makes an attempt to destroy everything about you.

I don't think we should be afraid. I've never been a devil chaser, neither am I a devil runner. When you are saved, you're sanctified and full of the Holy Ghost 1 John 44 says, "Years of God, little children, and have overcome them because greater is he that is in you, than he that is in the world. What's coming against me? The enemy. So often we get confused because we don't understand that we are simply under attack. For several months, our church was under tremendous attack. Once we had gotten out on the other side, we could look back and say, "The problem wasn't the seat I was sitting in, or that the building was too hot or too cold, or because of the songs we were singing. The problem was that the devil sneaked in."

Satan's Number One Weapon

When something goes against the grain, our mind's immediate response is fear. If Satan can put fear in you, then he has paralyzed you and can mess you up. Not too long ago I asked a family, "Are all of what you've had to deal with the last couple of months worth the pain you've gone through?" They said no, it wasn't worth it. I said, "Let me caution you not to fall into the same trap again."

The enemy will not stop fighting you until you have proven that you are going to stand firm in your faith. He's not going to quit trying to tear husband and wife apart until you have proven you're staying together no matter what. He's not going to stop trying to tear your children apart until you make him understand that come hell or high water, you're fighting for your children; because if you don't fight for your children, no one else will.

Every so often people come and ask me to pray for their son or daughter. I always ask if they have been praying for them. If they say no, I tell them I'm not going to pray for them either. If you're not willing to stand up and fend for your family, then don't expect someone else to. It is your responsibility. Now as a co-partner, I can pray with you. But I don't think God is going to take your slothfulness and bless you because of my prayer.

A preacher had been out on the road for several months ministering, preaching, and teaching the Word. Finally, he was going to get a break. He had preached his last night and was going to have a few weeks off to regroup. At about one o'clock in the morning his phone rang. It stunned him. He'd just given all he had to the Lord and was drained mentally and physically. But he began talking with the person on the other end of the line. This person poured out his problem and shared all he felt he needed to, that he felt like a failure, that the whole world had turned against him, and on and on and on. Finally the minister broke in, maybe a bit rudely and said, "Your problem is that you're under attack and you don't know you're under attack." Some people don't know how to recognize the attacks of the enemy. There are saints who have been besieged for twenty, thirty, forty, fifty years, wonderful people, but they are ignorant of enemy attacks.

In the church world today, there are those who don't understand. They have been blinded by the idea that if you just get saved, every-thing will be okay. When you get saved things will be better because your mind will be changed, but then you're going to have to work out your salvation.

Gift and Demand

Last year someone gave me a lawn mower. It was free, but I have to put oil in it, sharpen the blades, change the plugs, and put gas in it, or it is of no value. Even though it was free to me, I have to earn money for the fuel to make that gift valuable. When I got saved, it was free. Christ paid the price for me to be saved. But immediately after I was saved there came a demand, and that was to get in the Word and start learning. First and foremost, learn about your adversary. Learn about the one who is waiting at the back door of the church to mess with your head. You cried your eyes out and walked out the door a spiritually different person. Yet you get in your vehicle and immediately the devil says, "Nothing happened. You don't want to tell anybody about this." Have you ever been there? We should be careful not to act like we know everything, yet be ignorant of what the enemy is doing to us.

Many Christians walk around thinking that if they get saved, it's happily ever after, but after a while, it's kind of old news. I bought a new truck a while back and for the first three weeks, every Saturday morning I spent $3.50 to wash my truck. Now it hasn't been washed in several weeks and I really couldn't care less if it gets washed. The same thing happens in our churches. We get used to whatever it is that's going to happen and could care less if we miss or if we're there. It's just going to be another service; it's just going to be the same preacher.

Once, while we were having special mid-week services, I saw a family in town who hadn't been coming and I said, "We are having some great services." Their reply was, "Who is the big name speaker?"

3

I said, "He's the most awesome preacher you have ever heard in your life." When I told them it was our own Associate Pastor, they said, "Oh. Well, are you going to have someone different preaching Sunday morning?" We get caught up and allow ourselves to get into this trap. The evangelist is preaching and teaching the same word that our local pastors are preaching and teaching, but we'll get excited about the new man coming in. We get blinded.

Sometimes we get stale, and then we're looking in the offering plate to see what our neighbor put in. There are some who will sit in the back to see how much overall money is in the plate. "Well," they say, "What are they doing with all that money?" Sometimes we get so shallow, but not consciously. We didn't get out of bed and say I'm going to go to church and be shallow. We got out of bed and came to church thinking we were going to get something out of it, but the enemy is so slick.

If I let myself be distracted and blinded like the enemy wants me to be, then I can't teach and preach, and I sure can't pray for you. There is never a day that the phone doesn't ring with some negative garbage, so I have to spend time praying and seeking God and keeping my mind free because the enemy would like to come in and distract me.

I am writing on this subject for one reason only to help you become the kind of person who can recognize the wolf in sheep's clothing. No, I don't want you to be a devil chaser; that's God's business. But God expects us not to be ignorant. The closer we get to the coming of the Lord, the more the believer is going to need the Word of God. Jesus mentioned the devil often. He didn't exalt the devil by talking about him, He exposed the devil.

The Devil Made Me Do It

I have choices to make. People say, "The devil made me do it." The devil only makes you do what you let him make you do. He doesn't have power over you except for what power you give him. That's where believers seem to run scared. They think, "If I fast and pray and really get into this thing, the devil's going to fight me." No, time will come when he's going to have to leave you alone because greater is He that is in you than he that is in the world (1 John 4:4). We're not celebrating the enemy, we're simply exposing him.

You need the Word of God. Have you ever had your Bible get dusted over? People have asked why my Bible is so beat up. I have some brand new Bibles in my office, but the old one is my baby. Those pages just go where I want them to go. Over time, you mark Scriptures so that when the difficult times come you know right where to go and say, "God, this is what you said about the matter." When you allow the Word to become your helpmate, that's like saying, "God I'm taking you with me. I know if I'm in a financial jam, that Word tells me you're going to help me out. I know that if the enemy's coming against me and my friends are turning on me and about to break my heart, I know that you had to deal with the same thing. Lord, I need your Word."

Exposing the devil is not our priority. Knowing God is our priority. The more Jesus taught the Word, the more he exposed the enemy. The Bible lets you know what is to come. The Bible makes you under-stand that the devil is slick.

What did Paul say? I want ya'll to be ignorant? No, he said, "Lest Satan should get an advantage of us: for we are not ignorant of his devices" (2 Corinthians 2:11). He wanted believers to know that there is an absolute enemy out there, but the Word of God would deliver them, set them free, and set their minds at ease. You won't spend a more miserable night than when your mind is in shambles because of the enemy.

A while back, I had one of those nights. I was a nervous wreck, in a cold sweat. It was like a depression, a pressure. One of those times when you don't want anyone around. The longer I dwelled on it, the worse off I got. Suddenly the Spirit said, "Don't you under-stand? The enemy is messing with you." To myself I said, "Satan I bind you. I bind the works that you are seeking to do. I will not fall. I will stand in Jesus' name." Immediately, my mind was set free and my body relaxed. We need to learn to recognize and identify the enemy. And then we're going to have to understand how to take authority.

God never called us to be wimpy Christians. If He wanted us to just sit there and get beat up, He could use the rocks. But He gave us a mind and a spirit and arms and legs so that we could be about the Father's business. When people come through our church doors, God is helping me discern if they need to be around here, or if they are the kind of people we don't need.

For example, at one of our Sunday dinners, a visiting lady came in and put her arms all over me and said, "Ah, we're gonna have a wonderful time here." I thought to myself, I don't need this nut here. To her I said, "You need to be sure that you're here next Sunday morning. Don't miss it; put your life on it." When she asked what I would be preaching on, I said, "We're going to deal with the Jezebel spirit." She hit the door and hasn't been back since. You might be thinking that was a mean thing to say. But I already knew she had torn apart every church in the neighborhood. When Jesus found the moneychangers in the temple, he didn't say, "I know it's the Father's house, but we'll overlook it." No, He went in and He set things right (Matthew 21:12).

I have been criticized for speaking so bluntly. People have said 1 shouldn't be so mean in the things I say. My response is, "No problem. I'll speak to you the way Jesus did. He called people snakes and vipers."

"Well now, Pastor, that's not what I had in mind." I said, "Then exactly what did you have in mind?"

"We just want to come to church and feel good about this thing." There are sinners dying and going to hell because we're in our churches trying to feel good about this thing. The sooner God's people recognize what the enemy wants to do, the sooner they will stop criticizing leadership. I can criticize our state denominational office. I don't even know what for, but I can find something to fuss about. One day I called the overseer and told him we were going through this and going through that, and he said, "Praise God, man, you're doing good."

That was not the response I expected.

He said, "If the devil's leaving you alone, watch out. Don't you know the Bible says, 'Woe unto you, when all men shall speak well of you!'" (Luke 6:26).

I said, "We don't have to worry about that." Then you're doing good."

Who's My Enemy?

Too often, we can't fight the devil because we're fighting each other. That's because we don't know the Scriptures. Ephesians 6:12 says, "For we wrestle not against flesh and blood, but against principalities, against powers, against the rulers of the darkness of this world, against spiritual wickedness in high [places]." We wrestle not against brothers and sisters in Christ. We wrestle not against the music department. We wrestle not against the boss. We wrestle not against the vehicle. We won't maintain the vehicle, but we'll sure gripe when something goes wrong with it, and we'll come to church and blame it on the devil. Do you understand how much credit the devil gets even when he's not within a million miles of what's happening in your life? "The devil's got me hooked on this nicotine." No he doesn't; you got yourself hooked on it. I haven't yet seen the devil walk up to someone and put a cigarette in his or her mouth or go and flip the lid on a bottle and give him or her a drink. But we can sure blame it on the devil.

We are not wrestling against each other. We are not the problem. The enemy is the problem. Let's take Peter, for example. Peter did his best to keep Christ from going to the cross. Peter had seen Jesus. He had watched Jesus in the up times and in the bad times; and he had watched miracle after miracle. Then Christ began to lay out the Father's plan; another step, if you will; another chapter. In Matthew 16:18 Jesus said, "And I say also unto thee, That thou art Peter, and upon this rock I will build my church; and the gates of hell shall not prevail against it." Then you look down to verse 23, and Jesus turns to Peter and says, "Get thee behind me, Satan: thou art an offense unto me: for thou savourest not the things that be of God, but those that be of men." The Lord was telling Peter to shut up. "You're just letting the devil use you." One minute Peter's on the mountain, and the next he's in the valley. That" just like a lot of Christians. We can be on the mountain on Sunday, and then be in the valley Monday morning if we choose and let our minds go back to the negative.

What does the Bible say about the flesh and about your mind? Does it say, let it have its way? No, the Bible says you bring it under subjection. Mind you hush; you're going to think the way I want you to think.

People worry they will look foolish if somebody saw them talking to themselves. You'll look more like a weirdo if you claim to be Christ-like and say that Christ lives in your life, but you're depressed, confused, and cause more turmoil than a rank sinner. I'd rather look silly bringing myself under subjection.

It is our place; it's our job. The first part of Hosea 4:6 says, "My people are destroyed for lack of knowledge." One of the last things that Christ says in Mark 16:17 is that in His name they shall cast out devils. How can you cast out something you don't know anything about? How do you know what manner of prayer to pray? Does the Word not say to be specific? Petition the Father. We have to be specific and understand what we are dealing with.

Have you ever sat down in front of the television-just you, the television, and whatever program was on-and felt convicted about whatever you were watching? Do you know what that is? God is helping you to identify that particular enemy.

We must pray and seek God. Ask Him to help you understand. If you have financial difficulties, instead of blaming everyone, your prayer needs to be, "Father help me understand where the enemy is in my finances." Do you often have a bad attitude? "Father, help me identify what makes me have a bad attitude. What triggers me?" I like to fight and fuss because that's my nature. I have to fight myself and say, "God I don't want to go out there with my fist balled up." Often, when I come with a humble attitude, God shows me that I've gotten wrapped up with circumstances. Me taking the Scripture that says we wrestle not against flesh and blood, and putting myself in there to wrestle against flesh and blood.

Do you want to be humbled? Let someone treat you like dirt-spit on you, stomp on you, stab you, curse you. When you get a phone call that they are down, you'll see where you stand. I passed my recent test with an open heart, an open mind, and a willing spirit. I recognized that it's not the person, it is the devil that is coming against us.

If you're always tearing down your children and telling them how stupid they are, then stupid is what you'll get. "I didn't raise them to be stupid." Then quit calling them stupid. "I raised them to be kings and queens." Then treat them like queers and kings and maybe some day they'll catch on. If you don't grow weary in doing well, you'll reap.

A gentleman came to me and said, "Pastor, my wife and I are having problems. I just don't think we're going to be able to make it. I just don't see what I used to see in her."

Now this was my first (and last) counseling session with this person. I said, "What's her name?"

"You know my wife."

I said, "No, what's her name?" "What do you mean?"

"I mean the devil that you've got your eyes on who is about to tear your home apart."

"Well.......

I said to this man who was old enough to be my daddy, "You know, in your heart you're a wonderful person. In your heart the spirit of God is speaking to you to do the right thing; but that greed in your mind is going to destroy you. That greed is making you look like an absolute hind end. Your heart is telling you what you should do, because out of the abundance of the heart the mouth speaketh.

I was trying to help him see that the devil was working on his head. When I told him that, whew. One of the most difficult things you will ever deal with in life is truth. Truth. Solomon says, "Behold, thou desirest truth in the inward parts: and in the hidden [part] thou shalt make me to know wisdom" (Psalm 51:6). God says, "I'll teach you some things and bring some things to the surface, but first you're going to have to deal with truth."

If you've fallen into the trap of the enemy using you and using your mouth, be man enough, lady enough, to say, "I'm sorry." In Philippians 4:8, the Word says that if there be any good thing, dwell on, think about, talk about, desire, and meditate on that. It means changing, and saying "Lord, I recognize it's not my wife that was giving me the bad attitude. It was me being blinded to the truth."

One man told me that he likes a good fight at home, because after every valley there is a wonderful time on the mountain. I said, "You can love each other into those kind of times. You don't have to fight and bicker and make the neighbors wonder who you really are. You don't go out on Sunday morning as the man of God, and then come home and beat the tar out of your family just so you can have a good time on the mountain."

People are not going to accept me because I say I'm a pastor. They're going to accept me by what they see me do. The same goes for you. You told them you're a believer, but they're going to watch you and see what kind of fruit you bear.

A businessman in the community, whom I've tried to reach for four years, sat out in the church parking lot and said, "Pastor, I'm a heck of a lot better off than some people sitting in your congregation, and I don't know anything about this God you're trying to sell me on." I had to back off and say, "God, you know what to do when the church looks more like the world than the world looks like the world." The Lord said, "You're just going to have to start exposing the enemy. You're going to have to tell the people the truth."

If we can't stand a little bit of chastising, then how are we going to reproach a sinful world? How are we going to sell people on the fact that they need Christ if we come into our churches and fight, bicker, complain, grumble, and huff and puff and carry on so much that God can't even move. Then we go out and say, "You should have my God." They don't want your God.

But when your ministry, your church, and your family get linked together, then you're going to watch my back, and I'm going to watch your back. When the negative comes, we're not trying to tear each other down, because we stand by each other. We need to look up and step to a higher level. We need to grow up. Then we'll have something the world will want.

We wrestle not against flesh and blood. The enemy wants us to be blinded so we'll be discouraged, depressed, and so that we'll fall away, but we're coming together.

The enemy does not like you. Even if we don't want to mess with the enemy, we've already messed with him when we got saved. Now we're going to have to stand our ground and get bold and say, "This experience I've had with Christ is greater than any experience that 1 ever had out there. And I'm not quitting, I'm not turning, I'm not giving up. This is my God and this is my salvation. This is my peace and my joy. I feel righteousness, I feel the healer, I feel deliverance and I feel power coming in my life and the devil can't offer me that."

When you go to work tomorrow, and when you go home tomorrow night, understand that the enemy wants to tear apart those relationships. But don't be a devil chaser. Don't blame the devil every time something goes bad. If you run the tires on your car until the cords are showing, it's not the devil that made your tire go flat; you just ran them until they wouldn't hold air. If you run out of gas on the side of the road and you have to walk five miles to get fuel, that's not God's fault.

Let's be careful who we accuse. Let's recognize when the negative comes to us. Let's be men and women of God and say, "I don't want to hear it." Take that person by the arm and say, "My Bible says if you've got something against your brother, come on; let's go talk to him" (Matthew 18:15).

We have to be strong, but we don't have to be mean or be the judge. When something's wrong, pray about it. There are two different ways that we are attacked: one is by demonic influence, and the other is by our own ignorance. Decide which is what. Be careful. Put the blame where it is due. Ask God to raise you up to be a godly person.

CHAPTER TWO

HOW TO SURVIVE AN ATTACK

I'm a little disgusted with religion that teaches if you just get saved, everything else will work out. There are some things that we have to do on our own. There are some things that God requires. Salvation is free. Jesus Christ paid the ultimate price that we might have salvation. But I believe there is more to the faith than just saying, "Lord, here I am and I'm just going to sit here doing nothing for the rest of my life. I'm secure in the faith and that's it." We have the Word of God for a reason, and that reason is to read it. We have this privilege of prayer, so we should pray. We give of our substance, our talents, of ourselves, many, many times over, because Christ gave many, many times over for us. If we're going to be who God has called each of us to be, we are going to have to pick up the Word and get acquainted with it.

I understand that relationships are important. I understand that the workload is important. I understand that life is important. But all of those areas cannot function the way God ordained unless we first seek His kingdom. In Matthew 6:33, he said, "Seek ye first the kingdom of God." If I'm going to accept that word and begin to seek God's kingdom first and foremost, I must repent and understand that sin is anything that is contrary to God's Word. God has no part of sin, but someone had control of that sin. Someone put that sin on me. If I'm going to understand that, then I have to know there is a

God in heaven and a devil in hell. I have to understand that there is an enemy to my soul.

We have to look in the Scriptures and understand that we are not God. We are God's gift to a lost and dying world. We are vessels through which God chooses to flow. God wants us to go out and share the good news. How can you go out and share the good news if you don't know the bad news first? The bad news is that you have an enemy who is always warring against your soul. He is always warring against anything good. We must learn to recognize his attacks.

The first time you saw something in your home that was against the grain of what you believe is best for your home, how did you respond? Did you just leave it alone? The first time a child smarts off to you, it's funny, it's okay. But I guarantee that if they smart off one time and get away with it, they're going to smart off again. I'm not down on kids; I'm talking about being able to recognize things. I had a pastor once who tolerated a bunch of junk in the church. I didn't understand it for the life of me. I finally got bold enough to get in his face and ask, "Why don't you deal with this?" He said he was going to let God work it out. Because that pastor did nothing, he split the church wide open. As believers, we're going to have to learn how to recognize the attacks that come.

In the military, they practice. Some friends of mine have been in the Reserves. They tell me they get up early, exercise, work hard, crawl through the mud, sometimes eat pure junk, and tromp through the swamp. I've seen some scrawny looking friends join the military, but when they came out on the other side, they were men. The son of some friends of ours was just a boy when he entered the military eleven years ago. Today he is a man. He knows how to take his weapon apart, clean it out, and reassemble it. That weapon has become a friend. Could you imagine an army without a gun or a knife or a sword?

Can you imagine a believer wanting to go out and do God's work without a sword? The Scripture says that if you know the Word, in the time that you need something to say, the Holy Spirit will give you words (Matthew 10:19 & 20). But the Spirit cannot bring something to your remembrance that was never there. Often, we can't recognize an attack because we don't know the Word.

1 Peter 5:8 says, "Be sober, be vigilant; because your adversary the devil, as a roaring lion, walketh about, seeking whom he may devour." It doesn't make a lot of sense to me that God gave us his only begotten son, and that son gave his life on the cross and conquered death, hell, and the grave, yet I still have to fight for my life, my rights, and my beliefs. That's hard to understand, but it's something God did.

There is a reason God didn't do everything for us. If he just needed a bunch of zombies, then he would have used the rocks and trees. He wouldn't need us. But he gave us a mind, a brain, and a body for a reason. We are created in the likeness and in the image of God. We worship and honor the Creator when we recognize the attacks as they're coming our way. Are you fighting larger, bigger battles now than you did ten years ago? That's because you're stronger.

God is putting demands on His people. He is calling out a people who will be pure and holy and righteous. He's calling out a people in this last day who will make a commitment. God is about to pour out His Spirit in an awesome way. He's about to take the saints of God and lift them to a level they've never been before. But before He can do that, He has to get the six-month Christian as well as the eighty-year Christian to be wide-eyed and vigilant. Your adversary wants to mess you up.

The day you repented of your sins at that altar, wherever it was, you picked a fight. You basically stood up and said, "I tell you what, devil, I'm tired of the old life and I'm going to put on the new and you may as well face it." You spit in his face.

It's Time to Grow Up

What we don't understand is that as much as God's grace and mercy covers and protects us, God seemingly takes some of the grace and mercy from us at times. It's like when the little chick comes out of the egg. The mother protects it. What did the mother do with the egg before the chicken came out? She sat on it. Or like the mother bird who, after a period of time, boots that little bird out of the nest. Why? So that it will grow up. That's like taking grace and mercy. My Mom and Dad took care of me for a period of years and then one day dad said, "Go to work. You need to take those shoes you just cut up with your machete and replace them." You begin to learn responsibility.

It saddens God for people who have known Him for six months to be no better off than they were the first day. It saddens Him if, after twenty years, you're no better off than you were twenty-five years ago. He wants you to know the Word; He wants you to understand the attack. The enemy wants to tell you that you're not going to make it in the faith. God wants you to be prepared.

When is the most opportune time for the enemy to come to you? Immediately after God does something for you. There are a lot of things you can do in the natural that will protect you from being attacked. Be wide-eyed, vigilant, sober. Look around, understand. I'll tell you the way it is with me. I don't mind someone hugging my wife, but about the second or third time they hug her, I'm going to be watching how they grip her and how they treat her. In fact, I once told a man, "You can hug my wife, but you better hug her in Jesus' name, or I'll take you out behind the barn and whoop you." God gave her to me. She's my gift. My children are my gift. God entrusted them to me. I have to recognize when something threatens what God has given me.

Look around and when you see negative things happening, deal with them. If you see one ant headed for the garbage can in the garage, if you ignore it, in just a little while there's a picnic going on. If you allow one negative program in your home, there's another one on the way. If you allow one outsider to come into your home and treat it differently than you allow your children to treat it, it won't be long before the whole neighborhood is over. Why? Because there's a picnic.

God never called us to be weak-kneed. He never called us to turn a deaf ear. In fact, He expects us to be bold. We know that the military has the ability to fire weapons and missiles. We know that they understand when an attack is coming because they hear the bombs, machine guns, torpedoes, and planes coming. They know something's up when they hear the sirens blowing.

In the spiritual realm, when that Godly confrontation is coming, it is very much the same. Spiritually God will speak to you and say, "Something isn't right." Has God ever awakened you in the midnight hour? Has He ever laid it on your heart to get out of bed and pray for one of your children? It's like God comes and says, Knock, knock, knock. God will speak to you and tell you when weapons need to be drawn. He'll tell you when the Word needs to come to light. He'll speak to you.

Understand this, the enemy is always coming at you. But godly confrontation is when you recognize something's not right, and deal with it. If you sense that something is not right, get on your face and pray, "God show me. Don't let me fall into a trap. God you know the negative thoughts that are coming; help me to see the pureness, the light. Let me see the way I should go."

God will never call you to turn against what He is building. Lots of people hear the word confront and they think ball up your fist and fight, open up your mouth and hoot and holler, yell and scream. What is your first instinct when someone cuts you off on the highway? Do you try to speak all kind of languages with your hands? That is not godly confrontation. When you have to confront, if you're having to hoot and holler and scream, nine times out of ten that is not God working that thing for you.

We can look in the Gospels at the methods that Jesus used. Sometimes He spoke the Word. Sometimes He wept. Sometimes He walked in the temple and kicked the tables over. Sometimes He spoke with a stern voice. Jesus was the meekest man who ever was, but He was not a weak man. He understood the Word, He was full of the Word, and He was full of the Holy Ghost. He was full of power, because He was the One. People say, "We can't be like him." My Bible" tells me that if I believe, I can do the work that" He did, even greater works can I do (John 14:12).

I can take a good whipping as long as it is in Jesus' name. I don't mind being corrected, but no one is going to come abuse me and treat me like I'm a piece of dirt on the side of the road. I'm not dirt.

God made me special in His eyes. Sometimes we confront with a soft voice. And then there are those times when a situation is so far out in left field that we have to raise up a stern hand.

God wants to take His people to a place they have never visited before. But He can't take them until they understand that they can't just live off excitement. What's going to happen to your faith if you go to bed all excited and then wake up sick as a hound dog in the middle of the night? Then where is your faith? I can tell you where your faith better be. It better be for real, because God is going to allow all kinds of confrontation to come your way and he is going to allow you all sorts of opportunities to confront.

Recently, a gentleman who works on the horse farm behind our home decided he was going to stop and hang out over the fence while I wasn't home. My girls and half the neighborhood were swimming, and this man began to say all kinds of weird things to my children. For the next four or five days my girls wouldn't even walk around the neighborhood, they were so terrified of this man.

I didn't say a whole lot to my children, but when I heard that old truck coming down the road, I went out there and stopped the truck and the gentleman and I had a little chat. I didn't yell and I wasn't mean, but he understood that he'd better not fool with my children. He'd better not fool with my home. Suppose he had said those things and no one did anything about it? He would think he could come back next week and say something else. And after four or five times, he'd just be coming right on into the house.

You will recognize an attack because God's Spirit will say to you, "Something isn't right." When you begin to sniff out that something is not right, that is not the time to run. That is the time to anchor your heels in the ground and say, "I've got a war to fight. God's calling what I know to the forefront. He's calling me to be a warrior. He's calling me to take all of that training-when I've been dragged through the mud and gotten up early and prayed and cried and I've done all those push-ups-and to protect myself and my country." When it was time for Desert Storm we didn't need the military to say, "See you, I'm going home." We needed our military to say, "This aggression will not stand." us.

We must learn to recognize when the enemy is coming against

When we recognize that he is coming against us, we're going to have to put on the boldness in the Word of God and say, "Devil, you're not doing this to my family."

One time our family went to the beach for a few days. When we got home, my daughter Brittany's legs were so swollen, they looked like they were about to split wide open. I thought, "Lord, we had lotion on her. I didn't think she got that much sun." All the little hairs on her legs were singed off, like you'd taken a lighter and singed them. I sneaked in the other room and called the hospital and described her symptoms. They said, "Sir, your child's legs are burned and you need to get her up here before her skin begins to burst open." That just weakened this Dad's heart, and the compassion and the tears I'd been trying to fight off just welled up. We got together as a family, and we prayed. We love each other and we know that when one of us hurts, all of us hurt. Brittany was crying not so much from the pain, but she was praying for her faith. I've never seen a kid with faith like that. Her sister and her mother were crying too, and Dad was being as together as Dad could be.

See, I knew something about praying for a miracle. I remembered as a young boy, a nurse who weighed about 900 pounds carrying me down the hallway, strapping me down and putting needles in my behind because I was dying and eaten up with leukemia. I remembered a time when my family was walking out the door. I was doing everything in the name of God, and losing my family. When confrontation time comes, you need to remember the good things of God. Remember that your faith is stronger now than it has ever been. When the prayer was over, I took Brittany's legs and began slapping them. If I slapped her that hard right now she'd cry for six months. "Where's the pain, Brittany?"

"There isn't any pain, Daddy." And she got up and went outside to play.

When you put on the coat of righteousness, when you put on faith, the Holy Spirit will give you what you need to say and the boldness to take care of business.

Corinthians 13:11 says, "When I was a child, I spoke as a child, I understood as a child, I thought as a child: but when I became a man, I put away childish things." There comes a time in our lives that we have to stop accepting things that, as men and women of God, we need to confront. The devil will come to you and say, "God's mercy is so great and his grace is so wonderful. You know how Job suffered, so God's going to put sickness on you to give you more faith." That's a bunch of junk. God's not going to conquer something through His son who died a brutal death, who bore the stripes that we would be healed, and then curse us and put it back on us and say, "Now you're going to walk through it." The devil comes and says, "God's going to build your faith." As believers we know that God doesn't work that way.

People get upset in church and walk out and we say, "It wasn't God's will for them to be here." That's hogwash. If it was not God's will for people to come, they would have never walked through the door to begin with. We get blinded because of the attack of the enemy. The enemy sees a greater assembly coming together and he puts that child-like attitude on people. Because of pride and ego and other things, they won't make a wrong, right. The Word says when I was a child I responded like a little brat, but when I got full of the Word and the Spirit and began to listen to something other than my selfishness, 1 became a man. Now I understand that when hard times come, God is trying to say, "Son, there is another level for you." That's what He's doing. The more you come to understand these attacks, and know how to test the source that little voice that's saying, "God's going to bless you because you're so humble, so He's going to put sickness on you,"-you rebuke that thing.

I understand that there comes a time in our lives when it is God's will to take us home and that's it. But I also understand that the devil is going to put all manner of sickness and diseases on us. He's going to mess up our heads because he doesn't want us to know how to confront in a godly manner.

Through the Word, God will show you the enemy. He will help Through you discern the difference between right and wrong. He'll show you by His Spirit who is with you and who isn't. Have you ever had someone come up and start picking your brain and asking questions that are none of his business? You know he won't even get out of sight before he is going to be blabbing everything you shared with him. In your spirit, the Holy Spirit will say, "You'd better be careful what you say." A whole truckload of cord wood could walk through the door of our church, but if there is one wolf in it, my wife can sniff it out and say, "You'd better watch that one right there." She'll not say another word, but down the road she'll say, "Told you something wasn't right." Through the Word, God will help you identify and recognize the attack of the enemy.

When God helps you identify the attack, if you will listen to that voice, He will teach and instruct you how to respond. You can't always walk up and slap someone upside the head. For two years, someone had been against me. I know he did his share of slapping my name around the community. But in one of our services, I walked up and wrapped my arms around him and said, "I know I've hurt you somewhere down the line, but I want you to know that I repent and I'm sorry." I watched tears well up in that person's eyes and he said, "I accept." Truthfully, I shouldn't have had to apologize, but sometimes you just have to be the one to set the example. And then there are other times you're going to have to go in and push the tables over and say, "Okay, you pushed me to my limit. That's it."

God didn't raise us up to be ignorant. Don't let the voice of the enemy fool you into believing that God's not doing something powerful, because He is. Thank God for His Word, for His teaching, and for His special anointing. Ask Him to let that Word sink deep within our Spirits.

CHAPTER THREE

DEMONIC RANKS

I'm convinced that if the enemy is not constantly after you, you're not doing anything for him to be after you. If you say you care about your family, yet you never fight a battle and never go through the valley, then I'm not so sure what your conviction is concerning your family. I know when I stand up in all boldness and say, "This is the way it is in my home," seems an attack comes immediately.

It's time for Christians to get down to business. There are different ways the enemy comes against the believer, and we need to be able to recognize them. Temptation and wiles are two of the enemy's methods. The temptation is an attack that is very obvious. Sometimes it can be a distraction. One Wednesday night I tried to show our youth how easy it was to be distracted. I had a microwave and a small refrigerator on the platform. During my sermonette, I reached into the refrigerator, took out some ice, put it in a cup and poured myself some Coca Cola. Then I pulled out a bag of popcorn, stuck it in the microwave, and kicked it on. Can you smell that popcorn? In a snap, those teens were totally distracted from what I was trying to teach them. How easy it is for the enemy to mess with us.

The other area is the wiles of the devil. W-I-L-E-S. Those are attacks that are not so obvious. They kind of slip up on you, and you're sucked in before you realize it. Understand that as long as you're serving God, the enemy is always going to be coming against you. He's always going to be throwing temptation at you.

Another way to recognize an attack is to discern the level of your enemies. The devil has rank, order, and government. He has a system. He has a program. He knows that he wants to come against God's kingdom. If you're going to fight a case in the courts, you better have all the information together. If you're going to purchase a new home, you better have the paperwork in order. The enemy knows what he's doing. I'm not giving him glory, but I want to expose him. Sometimes the enemy is being allowed to work through people.

Jesus had to deal with that when He told Peter to hush in Mark 8:33. "You're not speaking the words of the Father, you're letting the enemy speak through you." Sometimes we need to be bold enough to say, "Why don't you hold your peace, because my spirit doesn't bear wit-ness to what you're saying." If we're that bold with our faith, we're going to lose friends. Is a friend a person who will allow you to lead yourself astray and never do anything to help you? Or is a friend a person who will say, "I will risk my friendship to help you"?

Ephesians 6:12 categorizes the ranks of evil spirits. It says, "For we wrestle not against flesh and blood, but against principalities, against powers, against the rulers of the darkness of this world. Against spiritual wickedness in high places."

Levels of Demonic Attack

There are different levels of demonic ranks that we have to fight. Every evil spirit has his own assigned position. Recently someone said, "You know, most ministries get hit with a single-barrel shotgun, but it seems we're getting hit with a double-barrel shotgun." You see, there are different ranks of attacks. There are ranks of deception, and ranks of friendship being broken, and ranks of homes being attacked. And if your home is being attacked, it's going to affect the way you worship.

And if we can be affected in the way we worship, then we're going to be affected in the way we're blessed, and then the church is going to be affected by the way we give. If the enemy can affect the way we give, that affects the church's ministries.

Sometimes we don't look at the big picture. When we're down on our spouse, if we would take time out to write down all of the good things and then talk about the one or two negative things, we'd find that the good is always greater. Philippians 4:8 says, "If there be any good thing, dwell on those things." But in our simple-mindedness, we pull out the bad thing and that's what we want to dwell on. The more you dwell on the bad, the more it affects you.

Principalities. Principalities are the forces and dominions that build nations and governments. That's their regime. The order of the government in a nation and the economy of the world can be influenced by these principalities. The enemy doesn't like to hear In God We Trust. In the early '60s, one person accomplished taking prayer out of the public schools. We let a congress say we want abortion in America, but "In God We Trust". Principalities attack in such a way that it doesn't affect one person. There's hardly a city in America today where you can't have an abortion. And that's just one subject. We should be a nation that prays for our leaders, that subdues the enemy, the principalities, and the demonic ranks, because whatever decisions our leaders make are going to affect us.

Look at the big picture. Look at the communist countries. We're quick to place blame on a person, but we're going to have to get off this person stuff. The Bible says walk in the Spirit. Galatians 5:16 tells us to get our minds out of the flesh, get in the Spirit, and understand that there are some things you can't fight unless it's through prayer and fasting. We, as a nation, can talk all we want, but when we go to bed tonight, all we've really done is talk. God's kingdom today needs more than lip service. If we're going to change what's happening to our nation, then God's people are going to have to come together and bind the enemy. The Bible says rebuke the enemy and he has to go in Jesus' name, but it's going to take more than one person to bind him (James 4:7).

Powers. Powers have authority to take action in any area that is open to them whatever entrance is given that will affect a multitude. The work of an evil power will be searching for an opening. How do you get sick? First you get the sniffles, then watery eyes, then a slight sore throat, then a headache, then achy bones, then a weakness, then a breakdown in the system. Before long, you've got yourself what we call the flu. Powers come and begin to pick apart. Notice I said wherever there is an opening. The Bible says in Luke 11:24 that if a person has had a demon cast out of them, that same devil will come back and see if there is a void in that spirit. If there is a void, it will get seven of its buddies and say, "Come on."

We want to do something for God and be something for God. We want to stand up and fight for our families. We say we are God-fearing people, but we don't understand that there are powers out there. I'm saved, sanctified, full of the Holy Ghost, but I can leave a void that the devil can come and mess with, if I let him. Key phrase, let him. That's why I try to get people to stand up, be bold, and come out of their shy ness. You're not going to fight the devil with a calm tongue.

That demonic rank in the spiritual realm is roaming to and fro, seeking for an area that can affect the whole multitude. He's not interested in you as a person. If he can mess me up, he's messed the church up. If he can mess you up, you've infiltrated the church. If you've infiltrated the church, then there's a multitude of people.

We take time to learn about each other, what we like and don't like. But we never take the time to learn about our enemy. How can you rebuke something that you don't know anything about? How can you recognize something you've never taken time to learn about.

Rulers of the darkness of this world. World rulers are evil spirits that govern the darkness and the blindness of the world that keep people from seeing wickedness and deception. These world rulers-these demons-want to keep you blinded. One of the greatest ways they keep the saints of God blinded is by always showing them someone else's sins, and turning their attention away from what's wrong with themselves. We say we know the Word, but we don't understand the Word. There's a difference. I can know about that motorcycle, but I need to learn how to ride that thing before I go out there and jump on it. These world rulers are always out there, not only to deceive you, but to keep you blinded from the truth.

How do you know when you're being blinded, or when these types of attacks are coming? When all you can see are the faults in someone else, the devil's taking you for a ride. The devil has taken me on one of those train rides many, many times. I'm not proud of it. I don't think I would have gone down the path I did if I had not been ignorant of God's Word. It was easy for me to accuse everything and everyone else. "It was mom and daddy's fault that I failed in business, and it was the bank's fault that they loaned me all that money that made me go bankrupt. It was never, ever my fault." That's what this demonic rank's purpose is, to keep you blinded. Understand that when all you can see is the bad in everyone and everything else, your arena has been silent for the wiles of the enemy, baiting you.

The enemy doesn't care if you fall in one day or fifteen days. He doesn't care if you fall in one year or ten years. He just wants you to fall.

The attack that you're feeling today may be the remnant of something that happened six months ago. But now that you're understanding that this is an attack, you can rebuke it, bind it, come against it, and the Bible says it has to go in Jesus' name. You can break that hold.

Spiritual wickedness. Wicked spirits operate from heavenly places. Their target, for the most part, is the church, and their method is wiles and deception. They are capable of planning fiery darts, onslaughts, doctrines of devils, and every false work or feat. It is no more than a wicked spirit if I went to Sister so-and-so and said, "Did you know about Brother so-and-so? Did you know what he was a part of?" That's nothing more than a wicked spirit. Planting that nasty, ugly, dirty thought, knowing full well that she's going to take it, think about it, mess up her train of thought, and then tell someone else. And she's going to tell it a lot worse than what I told her. Have you ever gotten in that circle? You said a five-word sentence, and by the time it got around it was a whole book. You started out in the ocean and ended up on a dry pond somewhere. These particular spirits, these wicked spirits, are there to continuously deceive. Have you ever been down and thought, "Okay, now it's going to be different. I'm not going to have it this way anymore. I'm going to change, I'm going to change, I'm going to change. This is it." You no more than made up your mind before that old ugly thought came right back, and that old wicked spirit came right back to say, "You can't make it. You can't do it."

Demons of low degree. These are the fifth type of demons. To be honest, they're stupid. They scream, holler, harass, aggravate, and mean absolutely nothing. My wife and I sometimes walk around our neighborhood late at night, and I'll tell my wife, "Don't talk real loud and let's see if we can get by the dogs tonight." Yip, yip, yip. The bark doesn't mean a thing, it's just a racket. There isn't anything worse than a bunch of gossiping Christians who get together and yip, yip, yip.

These little demons of low degree come to harass you. They take a headache and before you go to bed at night, you'd swear up and down you've got cancer or a tumor. They take a leg ache, because you've actually done some exercise, and before morning you're sure you're going to have it amputated. You've been there. The only power they have is the power you give them. The only way they can have dominion and run havoc over you is if you give in to them.

Look back at these five ranks we've talked about. Did you feel you've been attacked by the enemy at some point in your life? God's trying to do something in our lives. He's trying to change a people and He's trying to make us like Him.

If the demonic ranks can't destroy you with a harassing demon, then they're going to try to destroy you by the decisions the country makes for you. If they can't take you out of the church, principalities will take prayer out of the schools to affect your children. They get at you one way or the other. So what do we do, do we quit? Do we say, "It's easier not to hear the truth?"

No. I'd rather fight hell now than fight it later. I'd rather come together with brothers and sisters and say, "We don't all dress alike. Look alike, respond alike, and we don't all like the same food, but we serve the same God and we have the same identical enemy. So why do we want to fight the enemy through each other? Let's stand up as believers and say, "Devil no more! No more wicked spirits. No more powers. No more principalities. No more dumb devils. We have power over these demonic attacks. The God in whose name you can rebuke the harassing demonic rank, is the same God that will rebuke and come against the principalities from the lowest to the highest level. The same God, the same Christ, the same Holy Ghost. We don't have to change partners.

The high ranking spirits are very smart and they watch. They watch where you go. They watch what you say. They watch what you see. Let me put it in simple terms. I'll use the word hunk. You're trucking down the highway, and you look over and there's a hunk. You just about kill your crazy self trying to get a better look. The demonic spirit who has been assigned to mess you up will, just like in our military, go back to the camp to give a report. "Old Don Vining, this is what he's looking at and this seems to be his interest for the moment. Let's formulate a plan." That spirit comes back and next week there are three of them walking down the road.

Have you ever put one quarter in a slot machine? I guarantee before you leave you will have put every quarter you and your lady have in that machine. These spirits are not stupid; they watch you. Have you seen the plywood pieces people cut out and paint black to look like there's a man standing in the front yard with a pipe? That's like an old evil spirit, sitting out there unbeknownst to anyone, minding their manners, keeping quiet, but looking. We need to learn to register what we are seeing. We need to learn to come back to the camp and say, "Father show me what is of you, and then show me what is of the enemy." Then the Spirit of God will formulate a plan so you can attack the attacker before he ever launches that missile. Greater is He that is in me.

Symptoms of an Attack

When you are attacked, three things always happen. First, when people are under attack, they lose their spiritual hunger. Matthew 5:6 says, "Blessed [are] they which do hunger and thirst after righteous-ness: for they shall be filled." You can get up in the morning, dress the children, send them to school, go to work, come home and prepare a meal, try to get the children cleaned up and put to bed, and then, maybe, a time or two a week, come to the house of God. You can lose your spiritual hunger when you're under attack even though you're doing the same old things. You get to where you can take it or leave it.

When you don't pray, fast, and seek God, it can be months before you realize that you've lost your spiritual hunger. If you don't agree, miss church one time and see if the next time's not easier to miss. All I have to do is spend a day looking at the negative and I've lost my spiritual hunger. The enemy's job is to make you lose your spiritual appetite. So what do we do when we lose our appetite? Say: "Self, flesh, shut up.

You're going to get in the Word, and you're going to seek God, and you're going to hunger after God." That's why we have to learn to stand up and be bold. You can't come up against the sinful nature with a soft mind and a soft voice. There comes a time you have to stand up and say, "Hey! I'm speaking to you!" Be aware that when your spiritual hunger goes away, there is an attack underway.

Second, when people are under attack, they lose their strength. In Ephesians 6:10 Paul says, "Finally my brethren, be strong in the Lord and in the power of his might." When you're under attack, you lose your strength. You can't win if you are living outside the realm of the Spirit. As a Christian, have you ever felt weak? Numb? Sometimes, after I know we've been attacked, I ask my wife, "How are you doing?"

She'll say, "I'm numb." I understand that numbness. Sometimes we get spiritually numb because we don't know what's coming next and we don't know from where it's coming. We can get paranoid if we're not careful. When the enemy comes against you, not only will you lose that spiritual hunger, you lose your desire to eat. It's like when you catch the flu. Even though you despise the thought of food, you need to eat to regain your strength. That same thing happens spiritually when you're going through an attack. Your mind is boggled and confused, you're weak and don't have any spiritual hunger, and then somebody says, "What you need to do is pray and read the Word." UGH! That's that fleshly nature saying, "You don't want to do that!" That's that demonic rank, that little harassing spirit saying, "No, no, no. It will make you sick." You have to stand up and say, "I need my strength. Lord, even though I don't see it, I know I'm strong."

I have already come to our church like a whipped puppy, but when I started teaching the Word-even when I didn't feel like teaching the Word-something came alive in me. I regained my spiritual hunger. I lost track of time. I lost sight of whether or not I had eaten a meal. I wanted more of God because I had been reminded that I am strong. I'm not weak! I'd been reminded that I am something in Jesus' name. Be careful of losing your spiritual hunger, because that's when your strength goes.

A third way to recognize that you are under attack is that you don't feel like yourself. Something just doesn't feel right. I can tell by the way my wife responds when she doesn't feel well. When you feel out of sorts, take inventory. Remember, the devil is real. He hates you and me and what we're doing. He wants to wear down and tear up what God is doing at any cost.

Get involved in worship. Let's build up so much of the power of God in our churches that the devil does not have a chance against us. Instead of fighting each other, let's start fighting for each other. I'm nothing except that God saved me from a life of sin and I refuse to be bound. I was bound before I was saved, but now I'm set free. He that the Son hath set free is free indeed (John 8:36). I'm a free person. I'm free to shout, I'm free to raise my hands, I'm free to give glory to God. I'm not bound by cancer, by a headache, or by what the world says it wants me to be bound. I've been set free and you've been set free if you'll receive it!

The devil hates you. He doesn't want you to hear this truth. He doesn't want you to realize that you were set free at Calvary. We were whipped when we were sinners, but now we are set free! Oh, let that thought grip you. Praise God, by faith I have been set free. By faith I am somebody in Jesus' name.

When the enemy begins to plant negative thoughts in your mind, most always, it's a confusing thought. But our God is not the author of fear and confusion. He's not going to deliver you from a confused life and then tempt you with confusion. If I'm saved and know I'm saved, and if you're saved and know you're saved but are confused, where is this confusion coming from? Not from God. Remember when you first got saved? Remember the spiritual hunger? Remember the strength of the Lord?

What happened to your strength? What happened to your hunger? What happened to your filling? You used to smile. You used to be the life of the party. Twenty years later, some of us are just now realizing we've been under attack. You can break it if you'll listen to the Word. Pray. Renew your spiritual hunger. Let this truth seep into your heart. It will change you if you let it.

CHAPTER FOUR

HOW TO GO THROUGH AN ATTACK

Has someone ever accused you of having sin in your life because you didn't have joy and peace? Maybe it isn't sin in your life, maybe it is the temptations and wiles of the enemy coming against you to mess you up. I know from my own life that the devil likes to mess me up when I allow him an entrance.

The more you learn about the Word, the more you learn about the enemy, the more you learn about Christ, the stronger God's church is going to be. We are going to be able to weigh issues according to the Word and not according to the mind. I'm tired of trying to figure everything out. Should I buy this or not? Should I go here or not? I'm ready to get in the Word, in Christ, and hear that spiritual voice say, "No, don't do that." I'm ready to quit praying prayers that impress people and instead say, "You said you were my father, so I'm going to speak to you like my father. Father, I need you, Father, I need a word today, not next week."

When we understand the power that comes against us and the power that is in us because Christ is in us, we will know how to come against the devil. We won't have to say fifteen prayers and fast 9,000 meals for God to heal us of a headache. Now there are some things that go by much fasting and prayer, but then there are others that you stand up against and say, "Listen, I recognize you and you're out of my life now." We can recognize the enemy before he ever attaches himself. We can resist and rebuke, and in Jesus' name he has to go. We don't have to be ignorant of what the enemy wants to do in our lives.

Victory Strategy

Let's learn how to go through an attack. It's like buying a car. You get a vehicle and a thick payment book, but you also need to know how to make the payment. We know we have an enemy. We know there is a Christ and that we can be in Christ, but how can we be in Christ? We need more than a simple answer. We need to know how to go through the attacks of the enemy and emerge victorious.

First, understand that spiritual attacks will not go away by themselves. You cannot ignore a spiritual attack. You are going to have to do something about it. Recognize that the problem is not your husband, wife, child, church, job, cousin, parents, or car, it is the devil. You can't admit it is the devil, and then hush and not do anything about it.

We lived in an old, half-rotted-out wood home for about six months. At night, if we went into the kitchen and flipped the lights on, at least fifty to seventy-five roaches would scatter. The same thing happens spiritually. If you let that one devil alone long enough, he's going to get to feeling at home. He's going to invite his buddies in. If you let yourself tell one filthy joke, pretty soon there is going to come another filthy joke. If you allow yourself to spend finances in one area when you need them in another area, pretty soon it happens a second, third, and fourth time. Before long you are blaming God because you can't keep a roof over your head. The attacks of the enemy are not going to go away. God gave us a brain.

I make a conscious decision either to serve Christ or to deny Christ. We need to stand up and say, "God, show me what to do. Show me how I can deal with this." I found a local restaurant where I could order a big T-bone steak with a baked potato and a salad for less than ten dollars. The first time I went, it was wonderful, and I thought, "I have to go back." The second and third time I went back in the same week, it was wonderful. But when I went the fourth time, the steak was tough and I thought, "What has gone wrong?" Sometimes we take things for granted, and the whole time, the enemy is waiting to take us out of the spiritual and put us into the natural.

He doesn't want us to understand that sometimes we have to pray and fast. He doesn't want us to understand that our companion is not our enemy. He doesn't want us to understand that when we've worked out this difference in our home, we haven't conquered the world. There is another difference on the way. You know, you never lose until you quit. My wife and I made that determination about twenty years ago. If we fight battles for twenty years to get this far and then quit, then twenty years of our lives are wasted. If I decide now to get out of the Spirit and say, "I'm tired of the pain, the agony, the frustration, and always going through a battle," then the ten years I've put into the ministry would have been a waste. That would be like drawing a line in the sand and saying," Faith can take me no further."

You Can't Fight the Enemy in the Natural

I've noticed that the stronger the attack, the less I have to say. When people ask why I'm so quiet, I tell them it's because I don't have anything to say. I realize it is not my place to come against this in the natural. It is my place to say, "God, you said this battle is not mine; it is yours, but you're going to fight it through me." When God fights through you, it doesn't always mean that you're going to be doing something. Often, it means you are going to hold your peace and let the spiritual take place. When it is time for you to say something, you'll know that it is the unction of the Holy Ghost.

Not too long ago, my wife found out that some of her workers at the church weren't going to help anymore. Because she had had about enough, it was easy for her to want to blow her cool. But a phone call came in two days before that she didn't return. I said, "Go return so-and-so's call." When she got that person on the phone, the lady said, "God has been dealing with me about working in this area." No matter how mad we get, and no matter how frustrated and upset we get, God has already worked it out.

When we are under attack there is something we have to do, but that something is not wrestling with our brothers and sisters in Christ. Our place in this life is not to tear down who and what we can. The enemy wants us to get in the flesh and say, "Oh, I'd like to punch them in the nose." But all the while, God's spirit is saying, "Let me work it out." We get ourselves bound by a forty-year addiction and we want God to take it away in fifteen minutes. Let's give God an opportunity to work it out.

Christ had to go through spiritual warfare. Often, the devil will send a person who is going through an attack to mess you up. Even though it was the devil, neither person may realize it until it is too late. You may not understand that that person was under the influence of the enemy. That person may have been in the will of God last week, just like Peter, who said, "Oh Lord, you can build your church in me. You can touch me, you can use me, because I've heard from the Father." And Jesus Christ said, "You've definitely heard from the Father." But the next thing you know, Christ is saying, "Peter, shut up. You're letting the enemy speak through you" (Matt. 16:23).

One of the real dangers in our Christian walk is to think that we can get too good, too big, or too knowledgeable to go through an attack. God teaches us through the attacks, the valleys, and the upsets. If you don't know that a person is of the enemy at that moment, then that devil will send that person right back to you to poke you a little more. As soon as you understand and are able to identify different situations and attacks, you will no longer have to fight that kind of attack. Then the enemy will seemingly leave you alone for a while, until he finds someone a little closer to you.

I can prove it by the Scripture. The enemy attacked the ministry of Jesus through the multitudes and the religious leaders of the day. When Jesus remained unmoved, the devil tried to attack through the disciples. He tried through Peter and several others, and he succeeded in conquering Judas. Remember the story? Even though the attack came through one closest to him, Jesus knew the source and remained unhindered. He knew the goal of His mission and he kept

His eyes on it, even on the cross. In John 15:20 (paraphrased) Christ said, "They persecuted me, cursed me, kicked me, spit on me, and stomped on me. How much more do you think they are going to do to you?" If you desire the Lord to work through your life, then how much more do you think you're going to be kicked and spit on? How much more do you think your home is going to be in turmoil? The enemy knows that when there is truth and unadulterated unity in the home, there is a powerful force taking place. We're not going to give the devil glory, we're going to expose him.

We know he's not stupid, but neither are we. We have a God in heaven who gave us His word, teaches us His word, and causes something to come alive inside us. He will make us different-wise, knowledgeable.

Forgiveness Frees

When we go through an attack, if the outcome is going to be victorious for us, there's a very painful moment that Christ dealt with that we're going to have to deal with too. When they had Him on the cross, He said, "Father forgive them, for they know not what they do" (Luke 23:34). He could have had bitterness and anger and wrath. But at the point of death, He was willing to forgive. One of the greatest ways to shut the mouth of the enemy is to be a forgiver. In years past, if someone hurt my feelings, that was it. I never, ever, ever, wanted to see them again. If I saw them coming down the highway, I'd take off on a side street. I'd say, "I'm going to be a godly person. He said I have to love them, but I don't have to like them, and I'm not going to face them." I was hurt. Do you know that out of hurt, anger comes? And when you allow frustration and anger and hurt to grow in your Spirit, then bitterness sets in.

Bitterness Brings Bondage

Bitterness is like a cancer, it will eventually kill you. People ask if I ever have to deal with bitterness. Sometimes I'm so tired of the frustration, I feel bitterness welling up. Then I have to say, "No way."

When I see something becoming a habit, and when I see the enemy working in my life, I have to take a stand and say, "No bitterness." When there is bitterness, you can't forgive. We can't allow bitterness to be in our homes and in our families. I can't be bitter toward my wife or my children. Do they make me mad? Do they frustrate me? Of course; doesn't yours? But I'm not going to let bitterness in. Sometimes I go through a few days of being attacked before I recognize the symptoms. If you sneeze three times, you say "I'm getting a cold." In the same way, the second or third time something comes your way, in your Spirit you'll be able to say, "That's the enemy. I fell for that once before, but never again."

When we go through attacks, we're going to have to learn to for-give, Jesus forgave. He gave us that example. Of all the difficult times for Him to forgive, there was never a greater time than when He was hanging on the cross. Yet He said, "Forgive them, Father, because they don't even understand." That doesn't mean we look a person in the eyes and say, "I forgive you because you are stupid and don't know what you are doing." Sometimes we have to say in our spirit, "I forgive you." We may not like what that person is doing at the moment, but we can still love him and pray for him and care for him. One of the greatest attributes of being a Christian is a forgiving heart.

The devil hates it when you forgive. If I go to sleep after I've had a fuss with my wife, and I let it brew all night, in the morning it is sure enough going to be ripe. If we don't forgive, then in the morning we have to deal with the same junk. You don't want to get to the place where, when your family peeks out the window and sees you coming. They run and scatter because there is bitterness and anger and an unwillingness to forgive. Don't let the enemy use bitterness to eat you like a cancer. God is faithful and just. If you ask Him for forgiveness, He gives forgiveness.

Corinthians 2:10-11 says this: "To whom ye forgive any thing, I forgive also: for if I forgave any thing, to whom I forgave it, for your sakes forgave I it in the person of Christ; Lest Satan should get an advantage of us: for we are not ignorant of his devices." Let's not be ignorant. When there is an occasion to be hard or bitter, let's be the strong one and say, "I forgive."

You may have to forgive God because He didn't respond the way you thought He was going to, and you've been holding a grudge. You may need to say, "Lord, I don't understand all of your ways, and I don't understand how you think and why you respond the way you do, but God, I need forgiveness. God you know my heart and I know you've been waiting for this moment." Don't hold a grudge against our God.

Prevent Pride

To go through an attack victoriously, we're also going to have to guard against pride, a lot of great preachers have fallen because of it. Guard against pride because it will make you fight to show people you're right no matter what comes against you. People will even twist the Scriptures around to prove they're right. As believers, we often put on a spiritual front and allow pride to come and say, "I know how it should be and this is the way it is!" And all the while the devil is sitting back there watching. If he can keep us wrapped up in our own petty differences, we'll never find God's way.

Pride comes in several different types. There is the precaution complex. That's where every time something comes against you, you stand up and let everyone know you're right. We're not in this thing for a debate. In fact, the Word tells us about debating, fussing, and arguing about the Scripture in Job 6:25. We need to study the Word and find out what it really means. Matthew 6:33 says, "Seek ye first the kingdom of God." So if we seek God first, He's going to give us everything we want, right? I can guarantee that when you dig in and really seek his kingdom-you in God and God in you-you're not going to desire the pink Cadillac. Just because we are called and anointed, and because we accepted Christ fifteen or a hundred years ago, doesn't mean we're always right. The enemy wants us to think we are always right. But there is only one who is perfect. There is only one who is without sin. There is only one who has conquered it, and that's our Savior, the one we are striving to emulate.

After we've been attacked for so long, we can get the confrontation complex. After we've proven that we are right and we've taken all we can take, we're going to come out and confront. "I'll tell you who I am." Meanwhile, the devil is sitting back and saying, "They're doing this in God's holy name and they don't even know what's really happening."

I've found that if the devil can't drag you back, he'll push you overboard. If he can't push you overboard, he'll draw you out into left field. I went to a camp meeting wanting to hear one word: retreat. Give it up, quit, go on your way, dig a hole, dig a ditch, do something, do anything, go, go. I went to service after service and heard anything and everything except retreat. I wanted to retreat, to quit. I was tired of trying to change, tired of trying to make things happen. I'd had enough! It must not be God. Then I heard about what is happening all across our organization and among the Baptists, the Assemblies of God, the Methodists, the old time Pentecostals, the charismatic believers. God is saying, in a different fashion but in the same word, "Move ahead, march on, march ahead. I'm going to do something here; this is my time.

I've been under attack. The enemy wanted me to go into that precaution mode, to run and hide. But after we've hidden long enough, we realize there are spiders and roaches in that corner. Then we want to come out and come out fighting. "I'll show you in Jesus' name." The only kind of confrontation you better have is a godly confrontation. That's when the power and unction of the Holy Ghost comes and speaks, God said, "In the moment that you need a word, I'll be there" (Luke 12:11-12, paraphrased). Do you know why He said that? Because we'd goof it all up.

I once sat in the back of a church as a newcomer. I was considering going there to work with the youth, and I was scared. As I sat there, the pastor was doing his best to dismiss that service. My heart was pounding right out of my chest. I was seeing myself standing before the people, giving them a word. I thought, "Lord this is crazy." The preacher said, "Folks, I'm trying to dismiss, but somebody has something he needs to say." My heart was pounding and I thought, "Lord, if this is really you, let him ask again." About that time the preacher said, "Folks, I really want to let you go, but somebody needs to obey the Lord." I thought, You know, "Lord, if it is really you, I'm serious, if it is really you, let him ask one more time." I no more than asked God that, when the pastor said, "Folks, someone." Before I knew it, I jumped up and was up in front of those people. When I went back and sat down, I thought, "Man you are stupid. These people are old enough to be your momma, daddy, grandma or grandpa here and you're up there telling them what they need to do. When God moves you, you don't really have control, you go in Jesus' name.

James wrote to give us another foundation to win the battle effectively. James 4:6-7 says, "…God resisteth the proud but gives grace to the humble. So submit yourself therefore to God, resist the devil. He'll flee from you." John chapter 15 talks about being hooked up to the vine. Sometimes we think we are a special breed, but special breeds die off quick if they get unhooked from the vine. Sometimes we as believers, because of that satanic attack, get unhooked. But thank God because of His grace and mercy, if I realize I'm unhooked, I can hook back up. That's the great thing about this Christian life, this merciful life that He has given us. I can tell Him I'm sorry, and I can be restored. That's God's way.

A family that left our church recently called my wife. When they left, they were mad at me, even though I had helped them as much or more than I have any other family. When they called they said, "Sister Kay, we thought we were saved a year and a half ago, but we're in a little church now and we found out we weren't saved, but now we really are. We want to make our wrong right. It may take us some time, but we want to repay. We want the freedom to come and visit and not have to duck our heads and hide every time we pass the pastor in the hallway."

Sometimes it's so hard to stand. Because of the pain and agony of standing for truth and righteousness, we go home and wonder if the truth we believe is a false truth. The enemy tries to bind us in so many ways. But stand firm. Have a heart of forgiveness. It doesn't matter that we all don't think alike. When the enemy comes, don't run and hide in a corner. Don't let him push you until bitterness comes and destroys you. God wants us to be wise. He will be faithful to His word.

CHAPTER FIVE

WEAPONS FOR THE BATTLE

We must be changed because times are getting tougher out there. Have you noticed that as you seek to draw closer to the Lord, the enemy seems to get stronger? Many times, and in different ways we say, "I don't want to get any closer to God because there's too much pain. I don't want to go any further because it makes me change." What is Christianity if it's not all about change?

We are not in the compromise business. We're in a fight, a battle, a war. We're not ignorant of what the enemy is doing, and we're not going to withdraw from the battle. I'm going to keep marching until I hear that trumpet sound someday and the Lord say, "Son, come on home. The battle is over for you." If we really understand the Word, we know that the battle has already been fought. The victory has already been won. We may be struggling right now with paying the bills, an old car that isn't running like it should, and shoes that are wearing out. We all struggle. But when we begin to understand the attacks of the enemy, we can come out of that self pity and say, "I'm in a war because I'm a child of God, but I'm going to step up to the plate. The devil's throwing those fiery darts at me and I've run long enough. I'm ready for a change in my life."

Let's take a look at the weapons we have. We know there are different demons. There's the prince of darkness, and there are demons that affect our whole society. That's where abortion comes from, those powerful demons. If we ever want to break this curse on our nation, the total body of Christ must come together with prayer and fasting. Not two or three, but Christians everywhere are going to have to stand up and say, "I don't care if I'm Catholic, Baptist, Presbyterian, Methodist, Church of God, or Independent." God is tearing down those denominational walls and building up the body of Christ. There is a great shaking in the body of Christ. The devil is not going after the sinners, because he already has the sinners. He's going after the believers. God is allowing this shaking to come so that when the dust settles, He'll know who are His.

If we worship in Spirit and truth, then we have to fight the enemy in Spirit and in truth. We can't take a cowardly approach to the Gospel. We have to clean out that old way of thinking that says, "I've been saved for a hundred years and that's all the power I need." No, that means you've made a decision. It is a totally different thing to be in Christ, than to be of Christ.

Memories as Weapons

We have weapons to fight the devil, but Satan doesn't like us learning how to use them. He doesn't even like us to remember what we learned as a child, because he's afraid we will use it against him. That's why he tries to get us to lose our minds, so we can't remember something we learned thirty years ago that could give us enough strength to get through what we're facing now. There's power in what we learned as children. We didn't learn to write so that we could forget it someday.

I love operating machinery, but it has been years since I operated one. I said to my brother, "I could probably get out there on that 'dozer and really make a mess of things." He said, "Nope, it would be just like you were on it yesterday." That's something that is in me. When God is in you, God doesn't leave you. When there's a seed planted in you, that seed doesn't die. Even if you can't feel it, that seed is there. Don't look for a feeling when it is all about faith. You can strike that measure of faith and everything you learned as a child will come up in you and you'll say, "There is something there lasting that I never even knew." God's Word doesn't fade away. It's not like a fine steak dinner. I can have a steak tonight and be starving before six o'clock in the morning . But I can eat off the Word and when I get up in the morning, I'm ready.

Ephesians 6:13 says, "Wherefore take unto you the whole armor of God, that ye may be able to withstand in the evil day, and having done all to stand. Now that can also mean that when you've done all you can do to stand, when you're doing all you can do on God's behalf, He'll come in and make a way. God always, definitely, emphatically, comes in and makes a way where the enemy says there is no way. Look at this Scripture for yourself. Forget whatever needs you may be facing for a moment and feast on this passage. "Wherefore take unto you the whole armor of God that you may be able to withstand in the evil day."

There are several words in that passage that denote action on your part. Let's look at the word take. The Greek interpretation for the word take means strength. It describes the word as coming from the root of another word, insinuating the same strength as the thrust of a ram. You could easily read the passage this way, "Gather a thrusting strength to yourself through-not by, but through the Word of God so that you may be able to oppose, come against, and attack by overcoming and establishing yourself."

We must learn to read the Word, read the Word, read the Word. There is a reason you need the Word. The Word is a weapon. Acquaint yourself with Scriptures that deal with subjects such as faith, truth, healing, deliverance, prosperity, salvation, joy, peace, and soundness. If your mind is playing games with you, then get in the Scripture and find a word that talks about having a sound mind. If you're having faith problems, get in the Word instead of waiting for someone to come feed you, and say, "I need to know about faith." The more I dig into faith, the more I learn about faith. I have a worn-out little book called Precious Bible Promises. It is available almost everywhere. What's so special about this book? Glad you asked. If I'm lonely, I can look in this book and on page 156 it talks about Scriptures for times of loneliness. It lists verses like Psalms 46:1, "God is our refuge and strength, a very present help in trouble." John 14:1, "Let not your heart be troubled: ye believe in God, believe also in me." Romans 8:38-39, "For I am persuaded, that neither death, nor life, nor angels, nor principalities, nor powers, nor things present, nor things to come, Nor height, nor depth, nor any other creature, shall be able to separate us from the love of God, which is in Christ Jesus our Lord." There is power in the Word of God. If I'm lonely, I'll go to those Scriptures and I won't be lonely anymore, because I've found a friend and His name is Jesus.

We need more than a spiritual Band-Aid, something to make us feel better. It is one thing to know of the Word; it's another thing to know the Word. When you read it for yourself and research it, then you can say, "Ah-hah, this is for me." People ask why I don't get a new Bible. A new one is not marked up like the one I use. When I'm going through troubled times and my mind is numb, I can go through my Bible and find something I've marked in the past. It will enliven me and strengthen me with what I am going through.

The more you dig into the Word, the more power there is in what you're reading. The Bible is a powerful book. You don't need a psychiatrist, a counselor, an offering, another church, better music, or a new outfit. What you need is the Word. Psalm 119:105 says, "Thy word is a lamp unto my feet and a light unto my path." This Word will change your life forever.

Understand that when you let this Word go to your heart, the anointing of that word can fix your problem forever. I had read a certain passage over and over, but one day that Scripture jumped out and gripped my soul, and began to speak to my mind. I went to bed one night, tired and weary and heartbroken. My mind started playing games with me. I was a nervous wreck, but I began to pray. Ray. I told the Lord I loved Him, and I talked to Him just like I would to my earthly father. I told Him I didn't think I could take anymore. He reminded me that He wouldn't give me more to handle than what I could bear. People tell me I shouldn't talk to God that way. Yes, we should.

Don't you think God knows we are a simple-minded people? Don't you know that what we're touched with, God is touched too?

When we didn't have words, he sent the power of the Holy Spirit. When I don't know how to pray, when I don't know what to say, somehow the Spirit takes over and prays for me. I have a weapon that's not man-made. I didn't buy it at the store. I didn't pick it up at the post office.

Don't remind yourself too much of the bad times. Read the end of the book. I'm a winner, I'm victorious, I'm not going down. Christ is coming back for His church, and when He comes, we'll be out of here.

Ephesians 6:14 says, "Stand therefore." Now remember, the previous Scripture said, "Having done all to stand." God didn't leave us hanging. Understand that God will never leave you hanging. God has not brought you this far in your life to say, "That's it." The devil will say to you, "That's it, it's over, you're checked out." But God says, "*Wait a minute, am I not the creator? Was it not my breath that was breathed into your nostrils? Is it not my Spirit that made you a living thing? How audacious of you to listen to the enemy. He was once one of my chosen, but I beheld him fall like lightning.*" If you understand the Word, you understand that enemy of yours. Remind the enemy that you know the end of the book and you know where he's going to end. Can you see the flame?

Different Flames

There are two different flames we need to understand. There is the flame of the enemy-hell-and there's the flame-the torch of the most high God. There is an all-consuming fire burning in my Spirit. It's not a destructive kind of fire, it's one of those fires that build you up and make you feel forty feet tall. I feel what David must have felt. Is there not a cause here? There are people who desperately need Jesus.

Ephesians 6:14-16a says, "Stand therefore, having your loins gird about with truth and having on the breastplate of righteousness; and your feet shod with the preparation of the gospel of peace; Above all taking the shield of faith." No matter if your faith be great or small, above all take what God has given you, the shield of faith." Ephesians 6:16 continues, "Wherewith ye shall be able to quench all

44

the fiery darts of the wicked." All I have to do is take the faith that He has planted in me and I can reject every oncoming missile and act of destruction in Jesus' name! Have you ever shot a tree with a BB gun and the BB popped back and hit you in the forehead? Did you turn around to see how many people were watching? Or have you ever hit a golf ball and it came back at you? I guarantee it will break you from ever wanting to play golf. Use the shield of faith to send the enemy's fiery darts right back at him.

Verse 16-17 says, "Above all taking the shield of faith, wherewith you shall be able to quench all the fiery darts of the wicked, and taking the helmet of salvation and the sword of the spirit which is the word of God." But we don't want to leave out verse 18 which says, "Praying always with all prayer and supplication." Praying always. Not some-times, not every now and then, not when I'm in trouble, but praying always. Every day I've got to be praying. When I leave the office, I've got to be saying, "Lord help me make it home safe." Always praying. "God, I want you to touch my family tonight. Lord, protect." I have had people tell me they pray a lot but don't feel anything. Quit trying to feel your prayers. Instead, say, "By faith I lift them up and by faith, Lord, you're going to hear me."

God does not need you to tell Him the Scripture. We do that for our benefit. We can say, "Lord, remember Isaiah 41:10 where you told me to fear not?" That's a way to use your weapon. We need God's word to say, "Lord, you said I could cast my cares upon you. Lord you said you would break the yoke. Lord you said you would take care of my burdens." But we can't say those things with an honest heart and a good report until we know those Scriptures.

If you don't know how to pray, if you don't know enough of the Scripture to say it back to God, then all you really need to do is begin saying the name of Jesus, Jesus, Jesus, Jesus. Because when you speak the name of Jesus, every demon in hell has to go. They can't stand in the name of Jesus. They can't stand in that power. And after you quote the name Jesus, pretty soon you'll be saying, "I plead the blood. I plead the blood." Pretty soon you'll remember a Scripture you learned as a child, "The Lord is my shepherd I shall not want" (Psalm 23:1). Then you'll be saying, "God the Father, thank you for your son Jesus." See how it builds? In school you learned this, and then you learned that, and then you learned something else.

Look back at verse 15, "Having your feet shod with the preparation of the gospel of peace." If it says have your feet shod with the preparation of the gospel, what is the gospel? If this is something I'm going to put on my feet, I want to know what it is. I posed that question to the Lord seven or eight years ago and this is what He gave me. Romans 1:16, "For I am not ashamed of the gospel of Christ for it is the power of God...." Verse 15 says to have your feet shod with the power of God. When you put on the whole armor of God and when your feet are shod, you can take your hands and say, "I place the power of God on my feet." Now I'm not by myself, because every step that I take, every moment that I breathe, I've got the power of God with me.

Whatever you're facing, whether it be insignificant or a major mountain, take this Word to your heart and know that you're not standing by yourself. God in heaven, the One who gave his son Jesus Christ for you and me, is in you. Your feet shod, you're covered with the power. I have something on; I have His Word. I'm going to become a student of that Word. I'm going to dig into that thing and I'm going to say, "God let something step out. Let something get into my Spirit that has never been there before. Lord, let a new conviction come. I know that you are in me and I am in you."

God will make a way where there doesn't seem to be a way. God loves you and He's not going to leave you. You are not by yourself.

CHAPTER SIX

MORE WEAPONS

The weapons we are looking at are for spiritual warfare, but they are also weapons to help us in our everyday relationships. We all have difficult moments dealing with people-husbands, wives, children, the boss, the grocery store clerk, the mechanic, etc. We are fooling ourselves if we say we have an honest desire to know more about God, to get closer to His son, to enjoy more of the Holy Spirit, yet have no appetite for the Word. Saying you're a Christian without the Word is like saying you have an automobile without an engine. It is useless. It is useless for you to stand up and say, "I'm a Christian," but know nothing of the Scripture.

There is a definite difference in being of Christ and being in Christ. It's one thing to hold onto something somebody told me. It is another thing to respond to Christ because I have seen Christ. For many, many years when I prayed, I would look up and say, "Oh God, somewhere out there. Lord, help me, here I am." But when Christ gets in you, you no longer look like you're staring out into space; you say, "Father" because He is so near. I'm sure you've had times in your marriage or your relationships when, even though the other person was standing right there, you felt you were light years away. The difference is that when we come to Christ by faith, Christ comes to us by power.

God always takes the little bit we give and somehow pours so much more back in. After twenty years with my wife, I don't go to bed at night wondering if she's going to be there in the morning. I know she is going to be there. I don't wonder if Christ is going to be there, I know He is going to be there. It frustrates me to hear long-term believers respond like new Christians. It is one thing for us to say, "I know the Scripture. I can quote it." It's another thing for the Word to get inside-to go from the mind and get into the Spirit.

I'll be honest and tell you that years ago, I could never defeat the enemy unless the preacher was there. When I was struggling with a nervous condition, we lived way out in the Ocala National Forest. I said, "Call the pastor. Mama prayed for me, Sweetie-Pie prayed for me, everybody else we could call has prayed for me and it's not helping." In the shallowness of my mind, because of the lack of the Word being deposited in my Spirit, I said, "Nobody can touch me but the preacher." The preacher drove out twenty-five miles, prayed a simple prayer, and I was fine. My mind was trapped into thinking I couldn't touch God without someone else.

We can't allow our faith to be based on another person. In Joshua 24:15 the Word says, "Choose ye this day whom you will serve." Not what you're going to serve, but whom. Recently, my wife said something that would have offended me a few years ago. "I'd be happy if the Lord would come get me right now and take me." I said, "What about me?" She said, "You're on your own, bud." A few years ago I would have been offended and thought she didn't love me. She's found something in Christ-a love, a connection-that can't compare to the love we have for each other.

How am I going to fight the enemy when he comes against my finances, if I don't know what the Scripture teaches about financial blessings? How am I going to defend myself against the enemy's blatant attack on my salvation if I don't know what the Word says about the security of my salvation? How am I going to defend myself when the enemy comes to take my joy and my peace if I don't know what the Word says about joy and peace?

We must become students of the Word. Without the Word, we are shallow people. Hebrews 10:35 says, "Cast not away therefore your confidence, which hath great recompense of reward." What is your confidence? The preacher? No. Jesus, and another name for

Jesus is the Word. There is a great reward, the Word says, if you don't cast your confidence away. I get frustrated with leaders who tell you that if you pray a sinner's prayer, your problems are all solved. Friend, your problems have just begun. We wonder why a God of grace and infinite mercy would allow us to go through pain. I believe it is because pain strengthens our faith, and because the things I've walked through, I can help you through.

Before gold gains its worth it has to go through the fire. Are we not like precious gold in the eyes of our Father? He never said He would go around the flames with us, He said He'd go through them with us. The only condition He puts on our gaining understanding is to get in the Word and learn it. Don't cast your confidence away.

There are some people who can't worship God if somebody is sit-ting in their seat. Have you ever walked into a church where the names are right there on the pew, and if you sit in Sister so-and-so's seat, the Lord's not going to move that night? That's shallow. What we've passed off for twenty, thirty, fifty, seventy, eighty years as reli-gion has been just that-religion. We have to get rid of being religious and get down to being real. We must have that internal relationship with Christ; but that will never happen if we cast our confidence away.

I know that He is faithful to keep that which I've committed to Him (2 Timothy 1:12b). Ask yourself what you have committed to Him. Your life? Your soul? Your being? Every ounce of hope I have in this life is in Him. And by making that commitment, I have committed to going through the valley of the shadow of death. You can't just go through it once there is always a valley. When He takes you through this valley here and you whip the enemy, there may be another mountaintop for you, but hold on because you're about to go for another dip. Don't get discouraged in well doing. In Psalm 51:12, the Word says, "Restore unto me the joy of thy salvation; and uphold me [with thy] free spirit." The joy of His salvation is different than my joy. My joy is a smile. My joy is being able to say I can worship openly. My joy is being able to say I can pray. His joy is taking you through the fire and proving to the devil that you're going to stand no matter what comes against you. This is the joy of His salvation.

The Word as a Weapon

The very first weapon you must have to fight off the enemy is the Word. Now how will the Word help you in your relationships? It will help you be a little more calm when you should be, maybe a little more excited at other times. It will help you understand things that you've never understood. Perhaps it will teach you to speak slowly and listen. The Word can teach brothers and sisters how to love each other in spite of themselves.

If I want to fight off the enemy, I have to keep my candle lit. My spiritual candle can't burn unless I feed it. It takes a spiritual flame to come in and make a difference. You can't expect people to say, "I want more of what those people have," if there isn't anything to see. And the only way for there to be anything to see is for fire to come alive in every one of us.

There is a real issue with God about people being unified, in one mind and of one accord. That is when the great church of this day began. When they were all in one mind and of one accord, the Holy Ghost came as a mighty rushing wind.

The Power of Song

Some might have a problem with this weapon because you're like me and can't carry a tune in a bucket. You have to know the Word, because this weapon is hidden in there. Unless you get in the Word, you'll never know it's there. In Ephesians 5:18 Paul says, "And be not drunk with wine wherein is excess, but be filled with the Spirit speaking...." One of the reasons a lot of us can't get anywhere in life is that we are too busy speaking.

I used to come home at 5 o'clock, and if supper wasn't on the table, my wife heard about it. I called it speaking my piece, when really I spoke war into existence. When we see things that don't appear right, we ought to get in front of the mirror and talk to ourselves. Is there really an issue, is there really a cause to fight? David never fought until there was a real cause. He didn't jump up and say, "Well I'm going to go whoop somebody. I don't like the color of the shirt you're wearing." Nowadays, before I speak out, I ask myself, "Is it really worth it? What does it gain? What will the outcome be of what I'm preparing to say?" Before you speak out, ask yourself if what you're going to say will confuse or enlighten. Will it tear down or build up?

Read the rest of Ephesians 5:18-19. "And be not drunk with wine, wherein is excess; but be filled with the Spirit, Speaking to yourselves in psalms and hymns and spiritual songs" If we start singing spiritual songs like "Amazing grace, how sweet the sound," or "What a friend we have in Jesus," the whole atmosphere immediately changes.

If you go back to the Old Testament and get into a little book called Psalms, you will find that there are one hundred fifty psalms and hymns and spiritual songs that deal with every issue you will be con-fronted with in this life. David walked through the valley of the shad-ow of death, but he had a word. Do you ever feel that there is actually something good trying to come up out of you? Write it down. David began to write down what was going on in his heart.

God talks all the time. Sometimes we'll be going down the road and somebody in the vehicle will be yakking away and I'll say, "Hold it. Get a pencil. Hurry." Years ago my wife would ask, "What for?" Now she just grabs a piece of paper and writes it down. Sometimes the Lord gives me something, but I wouldn't know what it means. But several days later, God would remind me of what I had written on that piece of paper.

Speaking to yourself, that's a weapon. Listen to some of the things David said when he was hurting. "Lord, the devil or these enemies are all about me ready to consume my flesh" (Ps. 27:2, paraphrased). Or he would say, "God this friend I trusted wants to take my life" (Ps. 41:9, paraphrased). Or, "Break the bones of your enemies oh God" (Ps. 42:10, paraphrased). Then he would sing, "Bless the Lord, oh my soul, for you are very great" (Ps. 103:1, paraphrased). Or, "I will sing of the mercies and judgment unto you, Lord, will I sing" (Ps. 89:1, paraphrased). Or, "As the deer pants for water, so my soul longs for you, oh God" (Ps. 42:1, paraphrased). "Yeah though I walk through the valley of the shad-ow of death, I will fear no evil... for thy rod and thy staff..." (Ps. 23:4).

Do you understand how the Word changes your mind and your attitude? God did not give us the Word just for information, He gave it to us as a weapon. Don't leave home without the Word. It is a light unto my path, a lamp to my feet (Ps. 119:105). When turmoil comes, instead of singing, "Prop me up against the jukebox," we'll be singing, "What a friend we have in Jesus."

Healing Words

Not only must we have the Word, we must be able to speak sweet, kind, compassionate words to one another. What happens if we begin to look for the good in everybody? If we begin to speak spiritual hymns and songs one to the other, we shut the mouth of the enemy.

James 5:16 tells us, "Confess your faults one to another and pray for one another that ye may be healed." When I confess to you, I'm connected with you. When I begin to pray for my brothers and sisters in Christ, somehow they're touched. Then we have unity, and in that, healing comes.

"The effectual fervent prayer of a righteous man availeth much" (James 5:16). In Matthew 12:25 the Bible says that a kingdom that is divided against itself will fall. As individuals, we are a kingdom. If my mind is planning the next vacation or the next day out on the lake but my body wants to lie down on me because the Spirit is not leading me, then I am divided against myself. I don't feel like reading, so I'm not reading. I don't feel like going to church, so I'm not going to church. I don't feel like complimenting anyone, so I'm not saying a good word. Nobody shook my hand, so I'm not going to shake anyone's hand. Walk in the Spirit and you'll not fulfill the lust of the flesh (Gal. 5:16). A kingdom that is divided against itself shall fall.

In the same way, a ministry that is divided will also fall. If some give and others don't, it's divided. Nowhere in the Bible does it say to give what your brother gives. It said give and you will receive (Luke 6:38). For some a sacrifice is $1,000; for others a sacrifice is $0.01. It doesn't matter what the sacrifice is, give your sacrifice.

How do potentially great ministries fall? Because the people, in their minds and in their spirits, are divided one against the other. She wears red and I like blue. He likes old hymns and I like new choruses. When we are divided against ourselves, we can't function. If we are going to be spiritual beings, we cannot respond like fleshly beings. I can't be divided against my brothers and sisters. I can't let them carry the load.

Three weapons: The Word, singing spiritual songs and hymns, and forgiveness. How can you ask the Lord to touch you and your situation when you're praying with a heart full of bitterness? The enemy will not only divide your kingdom and tear you down, but he will cause bitterness to eat you like a cancer. In time, cancer will take your life. I can go to my brothers and sisters in Christ and tell them I love them, and confess my wrong thoughts, and let them know I'm praying for them, and ask for their forgiveness. Matthew 5:44 says, "Pray for those that despitefully use you." Lord, if they're in the wrong, you deal with them. If they're in the right, God bless them. Lord, I forgive them. Help me forget it and get on with my life.

These are three valid weapons to protect a home, a marriage, your children. You've got to forgive. You've got to sing that sweet little song to them. You have to give them a good positive word. You can't always tear down.

Go to the Lord in prayer and ask Him to deal with you individually. Pray, "Father if there is anything wrong in my life-and I know there is because there isn't anyone perfect-deal with me about it. Help me forgive and forget. Lord, give me a word and a spiritual song."

CHAPTER SEVEN

THE SOUL UNDER ATTACK

By now, we understand we have an enemy, and we understand that God has given us weapons with which to fight the enemy. But have you ever wondered exactly what the enemy is after when he comes against us? Is he after our joy? Is he after our churches? Is he after our families? Is he after our finances? What is the enemy after?

We can't really fight the enemy until we understand what he is after. He has just one thing in mind. There are a lot of areas he will come against you, but they all have one goal. He wants to get your soul. He doesn't fight you with lust just to get you to leave your family. That's an area, an obstacle, a missile he uses to get at your soul. He has one thing in mind. He could care less about everything else.

Our souls are what is either going to enjoy eternity in heaven or misery in hell. Suppose you have a physical condition. The enemy is not just trying to destroy you physically. He could care less about your body, because he knows your body is going to fail you anyway. The Bible tells us that our bodies are going to return to the earth (Ecc. 12:7). We should not be surprised that they are changing colors, becoming all deformed, and drying up. The enemy could care less about your body. He wants your soul. If he can eat you up with cancer, maybe there is some chance that you will turn your back on God and say, "Look what God did to me." Job's own wife said, "Why don't you curse God and die?" (Job 2:9). There are little demons running around today whispering in your ear, "Why don't you just give up?" You can't give up because there is a little bit of pain in this body. If we could quit and get by with it, I would have quit a long time ago because I hurt every day. But this body is just for a moment. The Word says to speak to yourself in spiritual songs and hymns. Not in your head or your heart, but in your soul.

Your soul is that spirit, that inner man. This body can die. This heart can stop. The blood can dry up, but the soul, the spirit is going to live on. That's why the Word teaches us that if any man be in Christ, he is a new creature (2 Cor. 5:17). It's not enough to know that the Word said this. That knowledge has to get down deep into your soul.

The Contest

A story is told about a contest between a college graduate and an eighty-year-old gentleman. Both men were to recite the 23rd Psalm and the one who recited it in the most elaborate way would get a big reward. The young man stood and began, "The Lord is my shepherd. He spoke so elegantly I mean, it was sharp. When it was over the people stood and clapped. He went and sat down, very proud of himself. The elderly gentleman was sitting on the back part of the stage. He had on his old overalls, he was filthy, be stank, nobody even knew how he was elected to be a part of that night. He looked like he should have been out feeding the hogs. He took his cane and spent seven or eight minutes working his way over to the podium. Where the young gentleman could stand so elegantly, the elderly gentleman was stooped and had to hold on. He stood there for several minutes, and then, without looking at any notes, he began to quote that Psalm. "The Lord is my shepherd, I shall not want...." The entire auditorium was spellbound. People's eyes began to fill with tears. "Surely goodness and mercy shall follow me all the days of my life..." When he was done, he made his way carefully back to his chair and sat down. The auditorium was silent. What was the difference? The young man knew the words of the shepherd. But the old man, he knew the shepherd. He knew whom he was talking about. The young man had learned this great work in college, this little fancy treat, and he thought he could impress the crowd with his learning. There are a Lot of trained and learned Christians out there, but if they don't know Christ intimately, it means nothing.

If you don't know Christ, and don't know how to get in Christ, you'll never understand how the enemy is going to come against you. He wants your soul. If he can tear your home apart to get to your soul, he'll do it. If he can cause starvation to come to get to your soul, or if he can cause your car to break down to get to your soul, or if it can cause your house to burn down to get to your soul, he'll do it. I promise you, he's after your soul.

Circling Buzzards

If you are wounded and that wound is left unattended, what happens? It gets worse. If an animal out in the wild has been wounded, the buzzards will follow it. It may take a couple of hours, it may take three or four days, but they're going to follow it. When that animal gets so weak that it can't get by on its own, the buzzards move in. Those buzzards had nothing to do with that animal's condition, but they did their part. When that animal got to where he couldn't help himself anymore, those buzzards came in for the kill and cleaned up the dead.

Spiritually speaking, when you are wounded-when you have a broken heart or some internal things that are wrong-be very careful. The number one reason we don't want to talk about our problems is embarrassment. I won't talk about what is wrong with me because you may think less of me.

Sometimes we won't deal with what is going on inside because we are fearful of the outcome. The enemy has been allowed to gain a foothold. I don't care how good a Christian you are, how much you know the Word, how many spiritual songs you know, and I don't care if your Mama raised you to go to church. At this point, that doesn't mean a thing. You can't live off yesterday. You can't live off the shout of last month. You can't live off the word you learned in Sunday school unless you take that word and use it. Fear sets in and we don't want to deal with things.

The first few years of our marriage, we'd be getting along fine, or so I thought, but about every six or seven months my wife would have all she could take. I would come home from work and she'd say, "I'm leaving. I've had enough. I'm sick of this and I'm sick of that." I'd say, "What? You kissed me last night and said you loved me and you're going to leave me today?" It took us several years to realize what was happening. My wife is not a fighter like I am. I love to fight. Win, lose, or draw, I love to fight. My wife's not a fighter. She would take things that ate at her and swallow them and leave things alone because she is very strong in that way. She can handle a lot. I can't. When I'm upset, people know I'm upset. When my ears start getting red, you better get out of my way, I'm about to explode. Well, my wife could take six, eight, ten, twelve months of it and then all of a sudden something would trigger her and she'd say, "Can't take it anymore. I don't think you love me, the kids are driving me crazy, I'm sick of this home…." We had to realize that it was a cycle we needed to deal with. See, she would try to tell me what was wrong and I always had the answer. You can tell me I'm wrong, and I can know I'm wrong, but I'll still tell you that you don't know what you're talking about, because of ego.

The Bible didn't say if any man be OF Christ, it says if any man be IN Christ. If you're in Christ, your ego goes and you're willing to be slapped around a little bit. I said to her, "Listen, it started off about every year this would happen, then about every eight months, then about every four, then about every other month." She was wearing the suit-cases out dragging them in and out of the closet. Our luggage is worn out and we haven't ever been out of the county. Differences would come and because I would not listen, I'd tell her where she was wrong and that was that. That was my attitude. I'm not proud of it. What I thought was being in Christ is so different from what I understand today.

Nowadays, on a regular basis, she'll look at me and say, "How are you feeling? What's going on?" And I'll ask her, "How are you feeling? What's going on?" We'll talk to each other, because I found out she is the best friend in the world, and I'm the best friend she ever had. We've allowed ourselves to become one. We are still becoming as one. She can scrunch up her nose, and I'll ask, "Okay, what do you have to say?" I know her and she knows me. She can look at me when I get out of bed and know that I've had a rough night and somebody is going to get it today. Or, she'll know I'm in a good mood by my appearance.

True brothers and sisters in the Lord can generally tell when some thing is up. You ought not hide your feelings. Instead you ought to say, "You're right, something is up. I don't really care to get into it, but I need you to pray for me." We become brothers and sisters. We become as one. We become best friends. In our marriage, I don't want to walk out every few months, and she doesn't want to walk out every few months, because we continually work at our marriage. Serving Christ works the same way. You have to work at it.

Day by day, week by week. You may get up in the morning and read some-thing you don't understand, but tomorrow morning or the next morning, something will come up that means something to you. You may say, "That doesn't appeal to me tonight." But dwell on what is being said, and before too many days are out you'll think back and say, "That's what the Bible was talking about."

The enemy hates your soul. Shame on the house of God when we are so busy counting numbers, counting money, building buildings and having programs that we never take time to dig in and help and love and care.

You cannot be demon-possessed if you are covered by the blood. But the enemy can cause you to deal with the same results of being possessed: oppression, depression, obsession. The enemy doesn't really care if he comes against you or if he comes in you, he wants to get at your soul. And if he can't get into you right now, as long as he is doing something to torment you, he'll be like the old buzzard, waiting and waiting. Some animals go out and chase other animals even though they know they can't catch them. But they chase them until they wear them down.

That's what the enemy does. He may chase us for years in some areas. Do you think the preacher who had a dynamic ministry just woke up one morning, the enemy came against him, and his ministry was destroyed? Do you think the marriage that fell apart did so all of a sudden? They already had problems brewing. Churches don't just wake up one day in a financial dilemma.

The enemy has been coming against our souls, and even though we have been religious people, we haven't been intimate with our religion. Often it has been because of our ignorance of the Word, because we didn't know. When I get in the Word, my soul is strengthened. Before, when things would come against me, I'd ball up my firsts and say, "Come on." Now I can stand and smile because I know who I trust. I know in whom I believe. I know that He is faithful and that what I've committed, He is going to keep. I know that He is working out Jesus in my life and I know that even though I'm not perfect, I'm a lot better off today than I was yesterday.

We cannot hear the unadulterated Word of God and remain unchanged. Once you receive the Word, chew on it for a while. We're saved, so we have an adversary. The only way we can fight the adversary is through the Word. And if we'll get in the Word and stay in the Word and sing our spiritual songs, and be forgivers, we'll all get to stand with Jesus someday. He'll never say, "Catholics over here, the Baptists here, the Presbyterians over there...." No, He's going to say, "Come on, my good and faithful servants" (Matt. 25:21).

CHAPTER EIGHT

KEY AREAS OF THE SOUL

There are five key areas of the soul that the enemy comes against. One is the will. Have you ever lost your will? I'm not talking about the will you make leaving your stuff to somebody when you die. I'm talking about your choice. And your emotions. The enemy will put you on an emotional hayride. He'll attack your intellect, and your imagination. When I was having very serious problems, I resorted to going to a $100-per-hour psychiatrist. I went twice. The last time I was there, I looked at him at the end of the session and asked, "Sir, will I always be this way?" He looked at me and said, "Son, that's really up to you. What I see is that you really need to learn how to control your thoughts." I never went back to him because I began controlling my thoughts. When I started having those stupid thoughts, I'd control them. The devil will take your imagination and come at your soul through it.

The devil will try to attack you through your memory. When you need a word, that word will be gone. If your spouse for life has told you you're loved, the moment you're hurting and have had all you can take, the enemy will try to make you forget about all the times you heard "I love you." He'll make you forget about all the times your partner walked through the valley of the shadow of death with you. There comes a time in marriage where you don't stay with the person because of the way she looks, cooks or acts. You stay with her because she walked through the valley with you for many, many years. She stood faithful. You know what she is made of. You no longer put stupid demands on each other. You say, "I'm so glad you're a part of my life."

It's time to be real with one another. Now when I read the Word, I'm going to read it not really caring so much if I understand it intellectually. I want my heart to understand. I want it to help feed my soul. We need to deposit the Word in our hearts so when the enemy comes against us, we'll have the resource with which to fight.

The Will Under Attack

If you take a slice out of a big old chocolate cake, it won't look as great as it did just a few moments ago. After it sits there for three or four days, it's not as great as it was three or four days before. Satan begins to tear you down physically, mentally, and spiritually to get at your soul. A lot of folks think the enemy is just trying to tear their bodies down. We already know where the body comes from, and where it is going. The outside is perishing, failing, and going to waste. Day by day we see something that is worse than it was the day before. Count on it. Accept it. But when this body goes back to the dirt, my soul is going to go someplace else.

I try to take care of this fleshly being through exercise. I sit down three times a day and exercise my elbows. I try to take care of my body, but I know someday it's going to be worthless. It's the spirit man that I am interested in.

Natural Temptations

The Word talks about the enemy in 1 Peter 2:11. "Dearly beloved, I beseech you as strangers and pilgrims, abstain from fleshly lusts which war against the soul." We know that there is a natural warring, a temptation, things you can see in the natural. If you drive by the car lot just to look, that's temptation. If you eat a forty-pound steak and then drive by the ice cream parlor thinking, I'm full, but I believe I can make a little more room, that's temptation. If this was a book on finances, I would say temptation is what gets us in a financial dilemma. Every so often, I have to sit down with my family and say "Okay now, we're going to turn these lights off. We're going to kick the A/C up just a bit. We're going to eat at home a few times a week." I don't think I am the only one who ever says we need to bring our spending back in line. We get into trouble because of the natural temptation, what the eye sees.

There is also the temptation to judge by appearance. There are folks who will not come to a small church because of the size of the building. "It looks like a barn. God can't be there." They see a fifty mil-lion dollar building on the side of the road and say "God is there." I've been in a few fifty million dollar buildings and the people were colder than a cucumber. But I've also been in very small churches and felt a warmth that I couldn't feel anywhere else. The enemy is always coming after you to mess with your head, to mess with what you see.

Then there is the spiritual, which you can't see with the natural eye. As I sat in a service one day, God began to deal with me about going across the sanctuary and asking an individual if he would like to go to the altar and pray. I said "Not me, God. They are going to laugh at me. I'm just a kid to them. Lord, I can't do that." Over and over I felt led, drawn to go. I knew I was supposed to go. I sat there and looked, and a gentleman from the other side of the sanctuary came over and bent over the other gentlemen. He couldn't have said more than four or five words before the guy jumped up and ran to the altar to get saved. God was trying to get me to stop worrying about what people would think of me so He could use me in the spiritual realm. God wants to use all of us in a spiritual realm. But we can't get into the Spirit until first we understand that there are some battles that we have to fight. God is saying that we are going to have to get into the Spirit so we don't fulfill the lust of the Flesh-what our eyes see.

Spiritual Attacks

The enemy not only comes against us in the natural; he comes in the spiritual. We can't see the spiritual with the natural eye. Our internal peace, lasting hope, and joy come from the inner man being touched by God's spirit. He is a spirit and those that worship Him must worship Him in Spirit and in the truth of His Word. The flesh is going to have to get out of the way. We're going to have to feed the Spirit, and it cannot be fed unless it is fed by the Word of God. That's why the weapons we fight with are through the Word of God. That's why our spiritual understanding comes from the Word of God. That's why the songs and choruses we sing are all fed by the Word of God. Everything leads back to the Word of God. The devil wants to mess me up, but it is not my mind he's after. I've been protecting my mind for so long when I should have been shielding my soul.

Spiritual Camouflage

The spiritual arena has often been camouflaged and ignored. It's been camouflaged by wonderful songs, wonderful messages, wonderful handshakes and wonderful ice cream socials. Often, we use camouflage because we are afraid of what is going on in the inner man. You see, when there is a weakness, it produces a fear. Have you ever had something going on internally that you were afraid to tell anyone about? The church unconsciously builds a buffer zone, because it is easier to make people feel better than it is for them to receive miracles. It is easier to say, "Come, and let's just pray a prayer. God bless you. You'll be fine now." It's easy because we can go home on time.

But when we begin to deal intimately with what's happening in people's lives, we may have to stay a while. For far too long, we've been promised things through God's Word without receiving the promise. If I tell my children I want to buy them an ice cream cone, they're not happy with the promise. They say, "Show me; prove it to me." A dozen years or so back, I was always promising my wife I'd get to that honey-do list. One day I told her I had good intentions and she said "Your intentions stink." That hurt my feelings, but I couldn't fuss because she was right. What good are intentions? The enemy is always coming against us and we're always finding ways to feel better instead of being better. I don't want my soul to have just another Band-Aid on it; I want Him to heal this thing. "God, I want to know the moment the enemy walks through that door. In my spirit, I want you to say, "Son, look out. The devil is here." You say God doesn't speak that way. I believe He does.

As a teenager, there were times I came home later than I should. My mother may not have dealt with me that night, but the next day she'd say, "God woke me up last night and I'm going to tell you what you were into." I used to think my mother was psycho, but then I realized she was just into God. That made me careful about the things I said and the places I went, because God would show her. "Behold thou desirest truth from the inward part" (Ps. 51:6).

We need to begin letting God deposit His word in us. Some of us have gotten upset with the bank because we haven't collected any interest. You have to have money in the bank to collect interest. We say, "I'm upset with God because I don't have any wisdom; I don't have any knowledge." Have you allowed Him to deposit the Word in you so that there would be wisdom? The enemy tries to hide these truths from us. He binds us by making us think that the way you build a church is by throwing a party. No, get on your face and pray, fast, and seek God and see what He would say.

Let's take a closer look at the five key areas of the soul: the will, the emotions, the intellect, the imagination, and the memory. We'll start with the will. Joshua 24:14-15 says, "Now therefore fear the LORD, and serve him in sincerity and in truth: and put away the gods which your fathers served on the other side of the flood, and in Egypt, and serve ye the LORD. And if it seem evil unto you to serve the LORD...."

Have you ever felt God was a little unfair with some of His demands? Sometimes it seems that everywhere you read-from Genesis to Revelation-you hear give, give, give. Give your money; give your talent; give your children. God says, "I'm going to bless you with a child, but give him back to me. I'm going to bless you with substance, but give it back." Give, give, give, give, give.

"Lord, you want everything and now you want what I've got." He says, "No, I gave you what you have." In the natural, it doesn't seem fair that I have to work as hard as I do and then give part of my money to the church. Remember we are talking about the difference between the natural and the spiritual. God said in His Word that He owned everything.

"…and if it seemed evil unto you to serve the Lord, choose." Notice how God also said to choose. We know in the inner man what we are going to have to choose, but in the natural, we fuss, In the natural it just seems evil to have to give away what we worked for. You mean I have to get up and help my neighbor when they are too sorry to get up and help themselves? Sometimes God will lead you that way to plant a spiritual seed. Somebody has to kick start us every now and then. We have to get into the spiritual to understand what God wants to say to us. In the natural, we can't understand that we're to bless the guy who just cut a donut across our lawn. I have to pray for that one who just cursed me? In the natural, that will mess you up. God has the Scripture the way He does, because He knows that without being in the Spirit, we'll never understand and it will drive us crazy.

But when we gain an understanding of the Word, we respond differently. The Word says, "if it seems evil for you to serve the Lord choose you this day whom you will serve, whether the gods that your fathers served that you were on the other side of the flood or the gods of the Amorites in whose land you dwell. But as for me and my house we will serve the Lord. And the people answered and said, 'God forbid that we should forsake the Lord to serve other gods. For the Lord our God, he [it is] that brought us up and our fathers out of the land of Egypt from the house of bondage and which did those great signs in our sights and preserved us in all the way wherein we went, and among all the people through whom we passed" (Josh. 24:15-17)

It's okay at times to question what God is doing. The writer here says, "You know, if it seems evil to do what God asks of you, then go serve your own god." I think somewhere along the line, some of us have decided to do our own thing. But after we live by our own personal gospel for so long, what happens? We come back from where God brought us. Then we begin to realize that the demands God makes of us are not so bad. If I bless Him with my tithe, He'll take what little I have left and do things I could never even dream of doing. When I look at what little I have to give compared to what

He gave, it makes me want to say, "God I want to protect my soul. I want to protect what you've given me. Lord, I want to get in the Word and see what I need to do."

The will is the dominant force of the human soul. It doesn't matter if you are born again or not, the human will has the final decision. God created humankind with a will because He didn't want a bunch of robots to serve Him. We would be no different than the trees in the fields. We would be no different than the rocks on the side of the road. But He wanted to create a people who could make a conscious decision to accept Him or deny Him. You're going to have to let the Word go to your soul and speak to your soul. Christ will show Himself to you. He will speak through the Word and wake you up.

Christ asked His disciples in the Garden of Gethsemane, "Could ye not watch with me one hour?" (Matt. 26:40). Can't you stay awake so I can show you the things of God? When we wake up, we have a decision to make. Do we serve God or reject Him? Do we have God as a Band-Aid or is He the sovereign God? It is our choice whether we go to heaven or hell. It is our choice whether to serve God or the devil. It's our decision whether to give in to sin or live in purity. Even after being born again, it is our choice to learn about the things and privileges of God. Everything in this life is a choice. God does not violate the boundaries He has set up. He's not going to make you worship Him. That's why the Word says to choose for yourself. If it seems evil, then choose whom you will serve.

There is a story about a gentleman who went to God and said, "I'd like to go to the cross warehouse and trade in this cross I'm carrying. This one is just too heavy for me." God said, "Go ahead and pick out another one." The man went over to a huge building, and there were tiny crosses, all the way up to crosses that would take a semi to move. He looked all around and finally picked out the smallest cross he could find hanging on the wall. He said, "God, I think I could carry that one right there." God said, "That's the one you were already carrying."

We have to choose whether we can carry a little bit of a load for God. Can we stand up and take a little pain for the one who suffered all the pain? Can we stand up for God and stand by God long enough for Him to change us out of the natural and get us into the spiritual? Can we give up our will long enough to see what His will is all about? I've never seen a person yet give to God and go to bed hungry. I've never seen a person yet who served and blessed God, blessed others, and took care of God the way they should do without. They may have valleys and tough times, but God takes care of them. I've never seen God's people take a family out of a tent and put them into an apartment only to have them sleep in the rain. That is not God.

The disciples asked," Lord, when have we ever seen you hungry and fed you? And naked and clothed you? And the Lord said, don't you know that every time you feed the least of one of these, you've fed me?" (Matt. 25:44-45, paraphrased). If you want to get close to God, quit worrying about all the other junk and just go out there and feed somebody who is hungry. God said you can't get any closer to me than when you feed the hungry, because when you feed them you are feeding me.

But we can't have that understanding in the natural because it doesn't make sense. It doesn't make sense that I can give, yet I receive. When we give, we are protecting our souls from what the enemy wants to do. We are setting up blocks. Same thing happens when we give our-selves to worship. When you sing a spiritual song, read a Scripture and allow it to get on the inside, you're setting up blocks and bars against the enemy that he doesn't know how to come against and doesn't know how to get through. It's all about getting out of the natural.

I'll tell you what keeps me going. When I get down, I can look out into the distance and see God. I'm not real sure how I'm going to get where He wants me to be, but I know every day I'm a step closer. I know every day something else is happening. Every day there is another miracle. Every day somebody is being saved. Every day somebody's life is being changed.

Have you ever gone out and witnessed and felt like you were nine feet tall? Have you ever stood up for God? We were in the grocery store recently, and a young lady maybe twenty years of age was ahead of us in line with her child and a cart full of groceries. After the cashier rang up the groceries, the young lady began digging money out of every pocket, her purse, straightening out dollar bills, looking for quarters and pennies. It didn't take me four or five days to decide what needed to happen. I just looked at the cashier and said, "How much more does she need?" I didn't say, "HOW MUCH MORE DOES SHE NEED-LOOK I'M ABOUT TO HELP HER." That's how a lot of people live. Look what I'm about to do. I shouldn't even tell you that I helped her, but I want you to know that when you are a giver God will turn it around for you. He may save your child because you gave. Somebody may not go to hell because you were a giver. The young lady didn't need very much, just a few dollars. I handed her the money and she looked shocked and said, "Thank you, bless you."

You know what I did that night? I didn't really feed that girl. I fed Jesus. And when I feed Jesus, my soul is strengthened. When the enemy comes against my soul there is going to be a reward, and God's going to say, "Because you fed me, I'm going to stand in defense of you and protect you." At times, God's going to say, "That decision you made wasn't the greatest, but because you are a giver and I know the truthfulness and faithfulness of your heart, I'm going to defend and protect you and walk you through this. I'm going to help you out of the mess you got yourself into." I'm talking about a God who will stand by your side. I'm talking about a God who says, "You can come against him, Mr. Lucifer, but you're going to have to come through me to get to him." I believe God is doing something down here. He is building bars of steel around us as individuals and bringing us together collectively. He is making something that will not be torn apart.

Battles? Yeah, there will be battles, but God's about to have a people who will smile and say, "I may be flat down tonight, but I'm going to be laughing my head off in the morning." We were teaching our children about tithing, and my little girl put a dollar bill in the offering plate and prayed, "God send me a baby sitting job." The next morning the neighbor called and wanted her to keep her kids for three days that week. My daughter came running to me and said, "Daddy, guess what I did?" "What did you do now?" She said, "I gave a dollar and asked God to give me a baby sitting job." Tell me that's not God. My wife came to me and said, "You know what that did? That built her faith." She did something on her own. She fed Christ. She said, "Lord, I'm not going to give just to receive, but I believe if I plant a seed, you'll bless me for it." You think I'll have to hassle her to pay her tithe on what she makes? She'll probably want me to bring her to church on Saturday. I'll be standing down there by myself singing a song and holding the offering plate.

The will has the final decision. Every other area of the soul will fail you, but the buck stops when it comes to the will. I don't care how good that cake looks, when the will rises up and says "no," that's it. When you're being tempted by the enemy and you know it, when the will jumps up and says "forget it," then you may as well forget it; because when the will speaks, the soul listens. When that mind begins to play games and tear down the structure of the soul, that will always jumps up and says, "Hold on, you're not going to be that way this time."

But from where does the will gain it's strength? If you sit home and watch all the junk on television, you can't blame God when you come to church and lust after all that you saw on television. There is a breakdown of the soul when we don't feed it, and the character of the will is broken. Just as if you don't give a plant water and fertilizer, it dies. That's when we say, "God, now that you're showing me something in here, teach me through your word how I can protect it."

Choose this day the direction you will take. We fuss at our old car when it quits on us, but we didn't tune it up for 900,000 miles and now we blame God. You can't blame God for decisions you make. The will is sovereign and God will not violate it. He will not come into that territory, you have to offer it back to him. When Jesus comes back and that old trumpet sounds, I want my soul to be cleaned up. Will you stay in the natural, or will you choose to give of yourself so God can do something with your soul?

CHAPTER NINE

THE WILL OF THE ENEMY

Not only does our will have the final say, but the enemy also has a will. Paul said, "I would not have you ignorant concerning these things" (2 Cor. 2:11, paraphrased). What he was saying in simple everyday street language is that we do not have to walk through life wondering what on earth is going to happen next. We can go through this life spiritually knowing that because of my will and my desire to serve God, it doesn't matter what comes against me. It doesn't matter who likes me or not, or whether I have a dollar or nothing in my pocket. My will is great in God and no matter what the enemy wants to do to me, God is greater. The word says, "Greater is he that is in you" (1 John 4:4b). I like to say it this way, "Father, let that which is within me rise up and be greater than that which is coming at me."

Sometimes I go through a battle and it's not really much of a fight. Then I go through battles that feel like the ultimate battle. Jesus said, "If I go away, I will send you another comforter" (John 16:7). For the disciples, it was a comfort to have Christ by their side. They could see him, touch him, hug him, eat with him, walk with him. They could even-when they stayed awake-pray with him. He was preparing them for His departure, but they said, "No way. You can't leave us. We have to live by what we can see with our natural eye." He said, "You don't understand. If I go away, I'm going to send you another comforter." He told them it was much better for them if He went away.

Miracles took place when Jesus was passing by, Miracles now take place when believers come together. The power of the Holy Ghost can be working in our churches here and can be healing people in Africa at the same time. Let the Holy Ghost rise up and be stronger than that devil who is coming against me.

The Fallen Angel

Isaiah 14:12-13 says, "How art thou fallen from heaven, oh Lucifer, son of the morning. How art thou cut down to the ground which didst weaken the nations. For thou has said in thine heart, 'I will ascend into heaven." Listen to the will of the enemy. At the moment you may not be the enemy, but with your will you can choose to be. If the enemy can get inside you by your choice, not his, then you can become the enemy just like Lucifer. It was his choice to become the enemy. "For thou hast said in thy heart I will ascend into heaven, I will exalt my throne above the stars of God, I will sit also upon the mount of the congregation in the sides of the north. I will ascend above the heights of the clouds, I will be like the most high" (Isaiah 14:13-14). He wanted to be like the most high..

Pride always comes before a fall. My pride goes before me, but soon it is going to cause me to fall down. The enemy was with God and thought he could overcome and overtake God's kingdom.

Just as we have a will, Satan himself has a will. God created him as a beautiful archangel, a chief musician. When Satan was in heaven, he led worship to the Father. But through his will he followed lust and pride and thought he would take over the throne of God. As a result, in Luke 10:18 it says, "And he said unto them, I beheld Satan as lightning falling from heaven." Just as soon as we set ourselves up to be some-thing we ought not to be, God has a way of bringing us back to where we should be.

By the enemy's will, he changed his status from Lucifer to Satan. God did not create Satan. He made Lucifer. But Lucifer, through a choice of his will, perverted his own destiny and is forever cursed by his choice. He is now Satan, the enemy of God and all humanity.

We have the same choice. Do we say, "God let my will be your will?" Lucifer decided he wanted more.

Isn't it amazing how some people who don't have a whole lot seem to get by with what they have? But with others, the more wealth they gain, the more they need. Wealth becomes a god to them. The more fame, talent, gifts, and friends they have, the more they want.

As the enemy made his choice, Satan was not alone. He had demons. One third of all the angels in heaven followed him. Willfully, the demons carried out the plans of their leader and vowed to fulfill them faithfully. A very familiar Scripture verse explains the will of the enemy. "The thief comes only in order to steal, and kill and destroy" (John 10:10 Amplified). He didn't come to have breakfast or to lay out on the beach. He didn't come to bring peace to our homes. He came to steal our joy and our peace. He comes against our will and begins to steal our direction. He doesn't just walk up and knock on the door and say "I'm going to take you out."

Spiritually Tuned In

We have to be in tune spiritually. The Holy Spirit will speak to us by our spirit and say "Beware, look out, the enemy is about to attack."

If you are listening to God, he will most always warn you before the attack comes. Then it is your own fault if you are taken by the attack. If someone proves that they want to be your enemy, they can't be your friend. We need to be careful with whom we become friends. I see many young couples come together, but the Bible says to be careful. "Be not unequally yoked together with unbelievers" (2 Cor. 6:14). The enemy cannot tear apart what God has placed together. He can hinder us and he can mess with us, but he can't destroy us.

Have you ever seen a good old boxing match? In our fight with the enemy, we may get knocked around a few times, but we just need to stand and hold onto God. We have to turn this thing around. When the enemy says I need to hate this person, I have to find a way to love him. I have to find a way to say, "I'm not here to be the judge. I'm here to be a friend." Granted, sometimes it is good to stand up with the voice of God and gently correct someone, but it is another thing to let the enemy destroy our will.

Aren't you glad that we have those weapons we talked about to fight off the enemy? Isaiah 41:10 says, "Fear thou not; for I am with thee: be not dismayed; for I am thy God: I will strengthen thee; yea, I will help thee; yea, I will uphold thee with the right hand of my righteousness." For so long I taught that one verse because it meant so much. But I slowed down one day, long enough to read what was being said afterward. God says, "Behold, all they that were incensed against thee shall be ashamed and confounded: they shall be as nothing; and they that strive with thee shall perish. Thou shalt seek them, and shalt not find them, even them that contended with thee: they that war against thee shall be as nothing, and as a thing of naught. For I the LORD thy God will hold thy right hand, saying unto thee, Fear not; I will help thee. Fear not, thou worm Jacob, and ye men of Israel; I will help thee, saith the LORD, and thy redeemer, the Holy One of Israel" (Is. 41:12-14). I like this part. This is why you don't have to worry about yesterday. God's going to help you chew up and spit out all those things that came against you in the past. He's going to help you get over them, and He's going to mend your broken heart. You're going to look back and do your best to hurt over that broken heart, but you won't be able to, because God's word stands true.

Verse 15 says, "Behold, I will make thee a new sharp threshing instrument having teeth: thou shalt thresh the mountains, and beat them small, and shalt make the hills as chaff." Like chaff, worthless. He says you're going to beat all those mountains that have come against you like they are nothing. All that stuff, all that junk, all that hurt, all those things that you've lost in the past are going to come against you, and you're going to chew them up and fan them out.

God said, "I'm going to make you bright, shining, new teeth. I'm going to pick you up and help you. I'm going to restore your mind and your spirit. I'm going to help you with what the enemy has done and I'm going to make you stronger than you were." Did you know that you can command the devil not only to give back what he took, but seven times greater? If he took your peace, you can demand your peace back, seven times greater. Read the Word. It says you will fan them and the wind shall carry them away. And the whirlwind shall scatter them. And thou shalt rejoice in the Lord and shall glory in the holy one of Israel (Is. 41:16, paraphrased).

We all have pain. Sometimes there is a piece of the past that wants to creep up on me, so I have to go to the Scriptures and say, "Hold everything. God said he was going to make bright new shining teeth. He told me that I was going to be able to stand up to the enemy. He told me that all that junk that had come against me was going to be as a thing of naught." I can't tell you how many times I've had to go off alone, pull out that Scripture and preach to myself.

The enemy wants to take your will by messing with your mind and causing you to forget what the Word says. The greatest weapon ever given in this life is God's Holy Word. People assume that because I'm a preacher, I know it from Genesis to Revelation. There are some books that I have a hard time finding. Does that shock you? But here's what I'm doing with what I am learning. I'm putting it to the test. In Malachi 3:10, God says, "And prove me now herewith, saith the LORD of hosts, if I will not open you the windows of heaven, and pour you out a blessing, that there shall not be room enough to receive it." God already knows what He's going to do. He already knows He's given his life for you. He's already given you hope that you haven't accepted yet.

The will of the enemy is to come and steal, kill and destroy. I know yesterday was tough. I know it is easy to get depressed. I know sometimes it's scary to know that you have an enemy and to know that he doesn't like you. But greater is He that is in you. Your faith is greater than anything the devil can bring against you. I got myself into so much debt when I was young that I had to declare bankruptcy at twenty-four years of age. It was hard. One day I decided that He had to be greater. I decided that if our home was going to stay together, I was going to have to change some things about me.

God is greater. We need to put Him first and quit trying to figure out His ways and say, "God show me the way. Lord, I'm not going to worry about how you're going to work this situation out; I'm going to trust you with my life. I don't have a lot of faith right now, but your word says that faith the size of a mustard seed is all I need. Lord, that's all I've got, but you said that is enough. Let this little bit of faith rise up and get stronger than that coming against me." Every time the enemy lashes out at you, God will be standing there saying, "Not this time."

God is one awesome God. Greater is He that is in you, than he that is in the world. If you are a believer, the Holy Spirit lives within you, and greater is the Holy Spirit. We need to learn to wait upon the Lord. Let's not talk so much about yesterday. Sometimes we have to reflect on yesterday, but we don't have to let it take control of our lives. I can't carry yesterday and tomorrow, plus deal with today. Let God worry about that. He can handle it.

CHAPTER TEN

A STRONG WILL MADE WEAK

The Bible gives us a great example of a strong will made weak by the enemy. Judges 13-16 records the entire story of Samson. The angel of the Lord came and told a woman that she was going to bear a son, and when he grew up, her son would deliver the Israelites. He would be special. The angel of the Lord also told her that Samson should never cut his hair. Unless God has told you that the length of your hair, or the style of your clothing, or the way you portray yourself is your strength, then your strength comes from the Word. We gain strength in God's name through His word. Samson had the same opportunity that you and I have. He could choose to let his will stay in the Word and be of God, or he could let his will be of his own selfish desires.

It is okay to admit we have been caught by our own selfish will. We receive much deliverance when we deal with our innermost parts and are willing to say, "God, I made a mistake." Even after Samson's rebellion, God still got the victory. Have you ever fallen down, goofed, and just made a mess, and then some super spiritual person told you were ruined, and God could never use you? You're just the person God can use.

Samson's Destiny

Think. If God were to come to us and say, "I'm going to use you to deliver my people." In fact, through the Word, God has come to us and said just that. He has chosen us to go out and win, seek, and save those who are lost.

God had a great plan for Samson's life. Samson had a wonderful childhood. He knew the will of God, and he knew that God was going to work miracles through his life. His mother and father knew that as well.

Samson's problem was not strength. He had physical and spiritual strength. His problem was that he loved women of the world. There are a lot of "believers" who love the filth and junk of the world. I have had people tell me, "I'm saved, but Pastor, I enjoy sitting down and having a beer." I don't understand that. I don't understand why, if God saved us, we can't let the things of yesterday go. I don't understand the faith of people who say, "He healed my neighbor, but I don't think he can heal me." A response like that could be a cop-out, or mean our will has been beaten.

In the story of Samson, we see how the enemy makes the bad look good. He never shows you the last chapter, he only shows you the beginning. Samson said, "She pleases me and that's who I want" (Judges 14:3b, paraphrased). I don't want what is good for me, I want what pleases me. Isn't that very much the attitude of the world?

Someone said to me, "Pastor, I've been in church for twenty years and I've been with my spouse for nineteen and a half years, and we just don't see things the way we used to see them. But there is this little lady down the street, we just see eye to eye. We are so compatible. Pastor, I think God's doing something." Wrong. God is not going to tear your home apart. "But I think I married the wrong one." Maybe you did, but God will make it right if you'll just stick with it. I believe about 90% of marriages could make it if they'd say, "I'm going to put my will in God."

Samson's parents had some questions. The Philistines were a national enemy, and the angel of the Lord had said that Samson would deliver Israel. Samson listened to their questions and then said, "I want you to go get that girl for me. She's who I want, she's what I want. She pleases me. I've got to have her. There's no other like her" (Judges 14:3, paraphrased). There's not another woman like her. There's not another vehicle like it. I've got to have that home.

The enemy is slick. It's just as dangerous not to have the Word, as it is to have the Word and not listen to it. If I go to church and do what's right on Sunday, but Monday through Friday I do my own thing, I'm a hypocrite, and the Bible talks about those kinds of people.

Samson's parents were worried. "Our child is a Nazarite and yet he wishes to marry a heathen."

I heard someone use an analogy when they were talking about becoming a hypocrite. A lady asked for prayer for her husband to stop smoking. The one she had asked to pray for them responded, "Have you stopped smoking?"

"I don't smoke."

"Well, is that your husband? Are you a Christian?" "Well...yes," the woman answered.

"Is your faith in God? Do you believe God heals?" "Yes," she said.

The other lady then said, "The Word says that two become one. If he smokes, you're a smoker. Tell God you're tired of being a smoker and you want Him to do something about it."

We are one in this thing called marriage. If one of us is suffering, the Bible says we all suffer. If one of us can celebrate, praise God! We all can celebrate. We are to be as one, but it is hard to be as one if you're going to marry a heathen. Samson's parents knew that. They also knew he was going to rebel.

Natural vs. Spiritual Thinking

It appeared Samson was going off the deep end. He married someone wrong for him. If you will just be patient and wait on God, he will send you the right person, the right vehicle, the right job, the right church, and the right ministry. It's just amazing how we as people who wear the name Christian-let ourselves get sidetracked. Whatever is going on in your life that is confusing you, it is not God. It's your will, your desire.

The mind says "just go for it." The natural will says "just do it. How can it be wrong? It will work." But God's will jumps up and says, "Hold it, there's a better way." God is showing me some better ways. I'm learning to say, "God don't let us have the will of Samson. Just because it looks good, don't let us just jump. Lord help us."

There is a difference when we go with Samson's will. I look good, I'm strong and fairly smart, and I know how to make it on my own. Samson knew how to go after what he wanted. I know God said to do one thing, but this is better.

There is a danger when we respond in God's name and don't sleep on it a few days first. If it's really God, it won't go away. Samson's mom and daddy said, "Son are you sure? Don't you want to think about this a few days?" He said, "No, I want her."

Well, he got her. He thought she loved him as much as he thought he loved her. It turned out she loved money more than him. It turns out that lots of people who seem so spiritual love the position better than they love the anointing. Being in Christ makes you act differently and makes you grow in grace. If you are going to grow in grace, you have to grow in virtue, faith, meekness, gentleness, patience, a spirit of forgiveness, and usefulness. To grow in those areas costs you something.

When the enemy comes against your will, he paints a pretty picture. He shows you what is nice. When you mention the name of God, there are people who will tell you quickly what they think because there are so many running around in the name of God. If you're driving a Cadillac, it's not going to putt around like a Chevrolet. If you are truly in God's will, somebody's going to be able to see where you've been.

Delilah said, "Come on, Samson, show me your strength." To him it was fun and games. It won't hurt to do this one time. He teased her and said, "This here is my strength." When she thought she had him, she called the Philistines and said, "Hey I've got him for you." Samson never even knew the enemy was sneaking up on him. He thought he was a tough guy, strong, a man of integrity. Armies hadn't been able to capture him, and wild beasts hadn't been able to overcome him. He played a game with the enemy. The next time, he told her something else and laughed about it. She said, "You've made fun of me." She batted those pretty little eyes and pouted, "Samson, why are you doing this? I'm your darling, your baby."

Just like that the enemy whispers in our minds and says, "Why do you want to give up this habit? You enjoy it, it's fun." I called an ad in the paper about a car. It sounded like a vehicle somebody could buy and maybe resell some day. I went over, and after about an hour of talking to the gentleman, I figured out he was a first class gambler. Before I left he knocked several hundred dollars off his price and said, "I want to sell this thing today. I'm going gambling and I need some money." That's no different than sleeping with Delilah. That's no different than hanging out down at the bar. Just one more drink. It won't hurt me. Just one more. I'm going to skip church one time. God won't mind.

Delilah didn't quit. "Come on, Samson, tell me. Where is your strength? I know God has given you this awesome strength, but come on and tell me." After Samson had messed with her head three times, she whimpered at him just right and he said, "Okay, here is my strength."

When we continue to do the same things over and over, they will eventually get the best of us. Eventually you will lose your strength. Very seldom do you hear a testimony of someone who has lived thirty, forty, or sixty years and never had to go through the dark valleys. I've been sidestepped and side tracked even though I didn't mean to be. The more money I was making, the more money I felt like I needed to make. It was okay to skip my tithe one time, but before long I could skip it two or three times, and it didn't matter. The enemy wants you to feel it's okay, when all the time he is tearing your will down.

His Choice

Samson didn't have to go through what he went through. You don't have to go through some of what you are going through either. Just back up and say, "God I want your will. I need your will." Samson gave in until he lost his strength. He lost his joy, his peace, his happiness, and his will power. Have you ever lost your will power? You got out of bed and went and laid down on the couch. I've been there. It's when you don't feel like mowing the lawn, you don't feel like going to church, and you don't want to go to work. You don't care about the kids. You wish your wife would just leave you alone. You don't want to do anything.

So often when we are under attack, the enemy is busy attacking our will. If you look back in Judges (22:14), the Bible says Samson's hair was growing back. And then a couple of verses later the Philistines were throwing a party saying, "Let's bring him out and make fun of him." There are people who will talk about you and make fun of you. They are going to make light of your faith. They've cut off your hair. They've cut off your strength. They've beaten and battered and tempted you until your will seems at its lowest.

Samson was at his lowest moment. They had cut off his strength and plucked out his eyes, so they had to lead him. He had failed God, and couldn't see spiritually. His blindness was symbolic of spiritual blindness. Have you ever been spiritually blind? You wanted to go the way of God, but didn't know which way was right. Samson remembered something. This is why it is so important to have the Word. Judges 16:26 says, "And Samson said unto the lad that held him by the hand, Suffer me that I may feel the pillars whereupon the house standeth, that I may lean upon them."

Samson knew he had wasted his life. If it turned out a blessing, why did Samson have to die? If his hair was growing back, which was his strength, and if God was going to come upon him one more time to destroy the enemy, then why wasn't Samson spared? Why did he lose his life? If you put the wrong junk into your system long enough, have an attitude long enough, live as a hypocrite long enough, play games with your family long enough, it will catch up with you. You can beat your kids to a pulp, but someday they are going to be old enough to stand on their own two feet. Play games with the house of God long enough. Put the right kind of chemical substance in your system, and eventually it will eat you like a cancer. Even though God will save your soul, you will have to pay for what you did to your body. I have some things going wrong with my body for which I have no one to blame but me. Many, many years ago a lady told me I needed to start learning how to work smarter, not harder. Samson knew he had let God down, and let his family down. He knew he had tied up with the wrong people, and ended up on the wrong side of the street. He said, "Lord, let me experience your mighty hand just one more time" (Judges 16:28, paraphrased). He said, "God, take my life. I don't deserve to live for what I've done to myself, but you, God, get the last laugh. Let's not let the enemy get the last laugh." God came upon Samson one more time and he killed more in that one moment than he did in his entire life (Judges 16:30). Sometimes our will is going to be challenged.

If we're not careful, we're going to fall. I don't encourage you to be a candidate to fall. But if you fall, let this word stand strong in your heart and your mind. Pray. "God, if Samson fell and you picked him back up, pick me back up."

The enemy wants us to believe when we fall, that's it. It is not. 1 have a choice whether I want to spend the next thirty-seven years the way I spent the last thirty-seven. Oh, my body may be down now, but it's about to get up. Why? Because my will says it's going to get up.

Ephesians 6:13 tells us, "Wherefore take unto you the whole armor of God that you may be able to withstand in the evil day, and having done all to stand." Outwardly, our physical strength can only stand for so long. We are only so strong, we can only do so much. But inward security, produces outward stability. When the trial, the fire comes against your will, you can stand. Do you feel yourself getting stronger? Be strong in the Lord.

CHAPTER ELEVEN

A STRONG WILL
KEPT STRONG

Samson chose to live his own life and do his own thing. In the end, he had to pay with his life. Now compare his life to Joseph's. Take a moment to read Genesis 39:1-23.

Joseph made some minor mistakes in the beginning, but he learned from them and turned them into godly strength. Making a mistake is not so bad. It's when you don't learn from it that the mistake becomes bad. A preacher once told me that if you don't learn what God wants you to learn the first time, you're going to go back through the same valley. Have you been through that same valley? By now, is your name all over the walls? I've been there a few times.

We make mistakes because we're not perfect, and sometimes God allows those mistakes to teach us humility. Someday we're going to be tempted with a great temptation and if we haven't learned from smaller, past mistakes, it will be easy to fall. God allows us those failures so we will learn from them. When a much stronger temptation, battle, or larger valley comes we'll be able to rely on what we've learned in the past.

In the first few years of our marriage, when bills came due, we'd go crazy. How are we going to do this? It's the end of the month and we just got over the first of the month. We'd write out all those bad checks on the thirtieth and by about the third week of the next month, all the checks were suddenly good. Then the next week it would start all over again. After a few years we learned how to deal with life. Being a Christian is all about learning how to deal with life. It's a hope, a peace, a joy we have.

Are you stronger today in the Lord than you were six months ago?

Do you know something more today than you did six months ago? I don't know everything and I'm certainly not where I need to be, but I'm better off than I was before. That's the way God is. He teaches us and helps us.

Faithfulness Despite Circumstances

In the Genesis story, we learn that Joseph had been sold into slavery. Right away, Potiphar, the man who bought Joseph, realized that Joseph had the hand of God on his life. When God is in your life, your neighbors know more about you than you think they know. They know about your faith and they know about where you stand. It's a shocker to be out washing your car and all of a sudden the neighbor you've never met stops by and says, "I'm eaten up with cancer and I understand that you are a Christian. I wonder if you have enough faith to pray for me?" People know about your faith. If you haven't been approached yet, hold on, there will come a day when that happens. What is your response going to be? "Um, let me go call the preacher." No, you have to be ready. You have to know that you have a measure of God's faith in your life. There have been times when I should have prayed, but I was scared. I didn't know I had the kind of faith that would touch somebody's life. But through the valley times, God has shown me that even if I can't go to the preacher for a word, God will give me a word. Because I have made an individual decision to serve Him, He speaks to me through His Word. The more He speaks to me, the more I want to know.

God will speak to you if you give him an opportunity. If you are battling with an area of your life, or seeking direction for a decision you have to make, begin to read the Word. Recently, I was sitting in our living room, and quite frankly, I was having all kinds of weird thoughts. I wanted to cry out to my wife and children: "I need somebody to care for me." I picked up the Word, and said, "Lord, wherever this book opens, I'm going to read." It opened right up to 2 Timothy chapter one, where Paul was talking to Timothy: "God has not given us a spirit of fear. He's given us a spirit of power and of love and of a sound mind." That passage began to speak to me and brought me peace. When you allow God to speak to you, he will speak peace to your situation.

Joseph obviously had the Word in him. The king said, "I'll turn everything over to you except my wife. I'll give it all to you. I'll give you control of my money and my lifestyle and my slaves." Often, the enemy will lie dormant and not say a word, not knock on your door, not say anything to you until you get up on the mountain. So many fine preachers have fallen when they rose to the top. Why does the enemy let you rise to the top before you fall? Not only do you fall harder, think what it does to those around you. The enemy knows that the more people you can influence before a great fall, more people are going to be hurt by it. People are watching us. If any man be in Christ, he is a brand new creature. He's not an old grump. There is something new, something exciting in him. Fall, the more

Joseph had a wonderful relationship with the people, but God was going to take him through some trials. In Gen. 39:7 it says, "And it came to pass after these things that his master's wife cast her eyes upon Joseph." Men, there may not be some woman out there casting her eyes on you. Ladies, there may not be some man casting his eyes on you. But there is some devil out there, be it a financial or an insane devil, who has cast his eyes on you. He wants you to fall. Someone out there is going to make an accusation to hurt you and mess you up. You are a believer and they hate the God who is in you, so they come against God by coming against you. At the end of the story, Joseph had to suffer because of someone else's lies and selfish ways. He was as innocent as could be, yet he suffered. If you have ever suffered because of someone else, you know that's when you have to be the great forgiver of the brethren.

Know Who You Are

"And it came to pass after these things, that his master's wife cast her eyes upon Joseph; and she said, 'Lie with me.' But he refused, and said unto his master's wife, 'Behold, my master wotteth not what is with me in the house, and he hath committed all that he hath to my hand; There is none greater in this house than I; neither hath he kept back any thing from me but thee, because thou art his wife: how then can I do this great wickedness, and sin against God?" (Gen. 39:7-9). There isn't anything greater than knowing and understanding who you are in God. Joseph said, "Hold on woman. I have control of everything in this house and I can have any woman that I want or desire. People practically worship me, I have the anointing of God upon my life. I know who I am." As believers we can look in the mirror and say "I know who I am! I know whose I am!" When you learn who you are, you respond differently.

People say I have a nice family. Of course, I have a nice family. I know who I am. I don't have to settle for junk. You don't have to walk around with your head in the mud saying "I'm a Christian, but I'm a nobody." That's an insult to God. That's like saying, "Father, I know you gave your son's life on the cross, but that wasn't enough. I'm still a nobody." He made you something! When you walk around with the attitude that you're nothing, you're cutting down God's creation.

Joseph knew who he was. I'm learning more and more who I am. I'm more than a pastor. I'm more than a husband. I'm more than a father. I am God's chosen. He has anointed me, called me, and set me apart. He has commissioned me to move out and make a difference in this world. I am somebody! You are somebody! Oh, if you can grasp this, you'll speed into your driveway and say, "Praise God, I'm some-thing! I'm somebody he can use!"

In Genesis 39:9, Joseph said, "There is none greater in this house than I; neither hath he kept back anything from me but thee, because thou art his wife: how then can I do this great wickedness, and sin against God? When you are being challenged in your faith, there are times you need to get in a corner by yourself and ask, "How can I do this against God? I know it seems good and sounds right and it would be a wonderful moment, but how can I do that against my God?" That's what Joseph said with great conviction. He was being tempted. When God delivers you financially, it may not be real smart to run right down to the car lot. Give God an opportunity. He might send somebody to give you a vehicle. Sometimes that signature cheats you right out of a blessing. I know what I'm talking about.

Joseph said, "I know who I am. I'm not interested in any more than what I've already been blessed and entrusted. Why would I have anything to do with you when I can have anything I want? Why should I sin against God?"

Joseph knew who he was. The Scripture tells us that the little lady came against him again and again. "And it came to pass, as she spoke to Joseph day by day, that he hearkened not unto her, to lie by her, or to be with her" (Gen. 39:10). Joseph had a made-up mind. We need to get a made-up mind. God has not given us a spirit of fear but of power and of love and of a sound mind (2 Tim. 1:7). I've had to make up my mind about some things.

Potiphar's wife came again and again, the Scripture says, and Joseph wouldn't listen. "Oh, come on. Come spend some time with me." That's like the little voice that says, "Oh, go buy that car. It's okay. You can make it. I know you only make $400 a month, but the payments are only $403. You can make it."

God is not going to bless you today and curse you tomorrow. That is not God. We're somebody. Joseph said, "Why would I want to sleep with you, when look at what God has given me?"

There comes a time when we have to know who we are. If the enemy comes one time and you defeat him, that doesn't mean the battle is over. It means you won that round. He's coming back. He's going to come back to see if he can find another area to mess you up. Had Joseph not been fused together with God's Word, he couldn't have withstood that temptation. Let me tell you about a king's woman. A king is going to have something that is absolutely fine. That's what Joseph was being tempted. Do you think the enemy is going to tempt you with a beat up something to drive around in? Have you ever noticed how you sit down and figure your finances and say, "Okay, I know we can afford $238 per month, but that's it."

You get out to the car lot and start looking around. "How much is this one? $316 per month. I think I can handle that." Huh?

The Bible tells us that one day, Joseph went into Potiphar's home and wouldn't you know it, all the men were gone. The only ones there were Potiphar's queen and Joseph. She went up and gripped him and said, "This is our chance, let's have a fine time." The Bible says he snatched himself and turned from her and ran. I believe he got way down the road before he realized he had left his clothes behind. The Word says he left her with his garment in her hand. Joseph knew when to run. He was not a coward because he ran. It was the only thing he could do at the moment. Sometimes, you have to run. Joseph with-stood, perhaps, the most trying temptation of his entire life. He was strong enough to say, "I won't sin against my God."

When you stand and say, "I will not sin against my God," the enemy will come a time or two and then he'll come out and make a last ditch effort. In Matthew 4:1-11 (paraphrased) Jesus had been fasting and the enemy said, "I know He's weak. Look here, Jesus, I'm going to give you the whole city." If the enemy would go after Christ, how much more would he go after you?

Learn who you are in God. Stand up. Square your shoulders and be somebody for God.

It is sad, but Joseph had to suffer because of someone else's selfishness. When the king came back, the first thing Potiphar's wife did was call for all the men and say, "Look what this heathen has done. He got me to himself for three minutes and tried to rip my clothes off and when I started shouting, he left his clothes laying on my bed." People will lie about you. Sometimes a lady will come and ask me to counsel with her. I always say I need to find out when my wife is available. "No, I just want to talk to you." Then I say, "I'm sorry, but I'm not avail-able." Joseph was thrown into prison because of someone else's lies. But look at what happened in prison. From the king's palace to the rot of the prison, God still gave him favor. No matter how low you get in life, if you are God's and you know you are God's, He'll still give you favor. He'll pick you up and say, "Come on. You may be in the dungeon, but I am your God. You may be weeping tonight, but because you stood strong, I stand with you."

Part of learning how to run the race that is set before us is knowing when to run and when to stay put. Sometimes we need confrontation. Jesus walked into the temple, kicked over the tables and said, "This is the way it is" (Matt. 21:12). Sometimes you have to be that person. Sometimes you need to say, "I've had enough of this company. I need to find new friends." Then sometimes God will let you help someone else. Everyone can minister to someone, but we have to know who we are.

The moment of trouble will pass, but the decisions you make will stand forever. You may be walking through a dark season, but be strong in the Lord. Stand spiritually. Tell yourself, "I'm somebody. He saved me and he said he would never leave me" (Heb. 13:5).

CHAPTER TWELVE

EMOTIONS UNDER ATTACK

God knows if the enemy can't get through to your will, he will mess with your emotions. Some of my most miserable days have been spent second guessing myself. As a rule, I'm not a second guesser. I make a decision and go with it. Because I'm not normally an emotional person, the enemy has used emotion to tear down my will to get to my soul. If he can get to my soul, then he can take away my hope. The most tragic thing we can lose in life is hope. When there is no hope for tomorrow, no hope that you can conquer, no hope that you can hold your home together, no hope that you are a person of integrity and can move ahead, then the enemy has you in a place where your will and your emotions are not where they are supposed to be.

I thank God that He confirms over and over that we are not here all alone. We are not on a downhill slope on a bicycle with a broken chain and no brakes. God knows right where we are. He knows what is happening.

Just as God has given us a will, he has given us emotions. The emotional side of humankind is a world all its own. Probably not a popular saying, but trust me, emotions can mess you up.

In the past, due to lack of knowledge, the church was widely led by its emotions. Because of this error, many were taught that it was not scriptural to feel anything, or if you did feel something, say you didn't. You can't take a broken heart and hide it for years and years. Eventually, it's going to get the best of you.

Undercover Emotions

I believe that 80% of the physical problems of the American people are due to the fact that they won't deal with what is going on in their inner man. Men are taught not to shed a tear. You stand up strong, even though you are crushed on the inside. You just put on a big smile and walk as a person of integrity. Ladies are taught, as mothers, to go into the bed chamber or into the closet, cry it out and then come out and say "Praise God." We are never taught to come together as believers and say, "I'm hurting, and I need somebody to help me."

There comes a time when everybody needs a shoulder to cry on. That's what the Christian walk is supposed to be about. We should be able to come together as brothers and sisters in Christ and cry on each other's shoulders. If the enemy can't tear down your will, he will go after your emotions. It doesn't matter what your personality is. We must deal with our emotions.

It is not wrong to have emotions. It is wrong to have your emotions out of control. Remember Peter? In Matthew 16:22, Jesus was telling the disciples things that were about to happen and Peter got all emotional. "No, how can this be?" Same thing happened in Exodus. God went to Moses and said, "This is what I want you to do for me. I'm tired of my children being bound and I've chosen you." Moses got all emotional, and the Lord finally had to set him straight (Ex. 3:6).

Sometimes we have an obligation to sit folks down and say, "1 need to set you straight. I need to help you get control of your emotions. You can't make decisions when you are upset. When you are mad at your old car because it didn't bring you to work this morning. Don't go buy a new car this afternoon. Sleep on it a night or two. When you are upset with your spouse because he didn't mow the yard the way he should, or she didn't cook the meal she should have, don't leave. Hold on, sleep on it for a night or two. Dinner will be there tomorrow night and the lawn will be cut before Saturday.

Statistics tell us that 50% of marriages in America will end in divorce. Fifty percent! That means if there are ten marriages repre-sent-ed by those statistics, five will end in divorce. That is sicken-ing, and it's sad. People get emotional and let their emotions get out of control. We must not make decisions when our emotions are all shook up.

Ask God to teach you when you are an emotional wreck. I'll tell you what has helped my wife and me make it for twenty years-it surely hasn't been because I'm a good guy. We have learned that when one of us is a bit emotional, leave it alone. Sometimes you just need to leave it alone and let it work out. Give it some breathing room. Let time begin to heal the emotions.

Controlling Emotions

God gave us emotions, but we are not to use them to manipulate or control another person. I'm sure you've seen people who can shed crocodile tears on command. God did not give us emotions to use in that fashion. I have had people come by my office carrying their little New Testaments and shedding those crocodile tears, telling me what a wonderful believer in Christ they are, but they smell like they just came out of the liquor store. People will use their emotions on you. When you allow yourself to be identified as a believer and the community knows it, they are going to come to you. Believers in our society are known to be "weak kneed." Jesus was humble, kind, compassionate, and He would shed a tear. He ate with the beggars. People think believers are emotional wrecks, easy to manipulate. It is sad, but in the house of God there are people who will use their emotions to manipulate. We need to be careful. We need to ask the Lord to help us use our emotions the right way and to give us wis-dom to discern when someone is pulling an emotional trick on us. Very simply pray, "Lord teach me what is real."

Our emotions were not made to rule us, they were made to enhance us. They were made to help us. Just as with the rest of the soul, the emotions must be matured through the Word of God. If you are having trouble with your emotions, get out of bed twenty minutes earlier every morning and spend time reading the Word. If you read something and it doesn't make sense, keep reading. You're on the right track and God's going to put something out there for you. When you get in the Word, and begin to meditate on what God is saying, He will settle your emotions. He will teach you and help you deal with things.

Wrong emotions have the potential to steal your destiny for God. Our emotions must be steered and guided. When emotions manifest, they must have a purpose behind them. When our inner man-our soul-guides our emotions, great results are produced. When we come into the house of God and say, "Lord teach me," we're not saying teach this flesh, we're saying teach this spirit. For they that worship him must worship him in spirit and in truth (John 4:24). My spirit must be truthful with His spirit. He is not some faraway God. Sometimes we get emotional and feel like God is not within 40,000 miles, only to find out He was right there.

I had a meeting scheduled with a gentleman whose ministry I greatly respected. I prayed, "Lord, let this person have a Word for me." I just knew God was going to give me a Word. Thirty minutes before the meeting, the gentleman called and canceled. Immediately the enemy came to my will and said, "See, God's not going to speak to you." That night I sat reading my Bible and a Scripture kept going over and over in my mind. Sometimes we need to say to our emotions, "Just hush up for a moment, I want to hear what the Spirit is saying." The Spirit was saying the Scripture over and over. As I began to get into it, I realized it was a much greater word than that gentleman could ever have given me. I may be walking through the valley of the shadow of death, but God can speak to me and it will have a greater impact than any man's word. It will make a difference in my life.

Emotional Sources

When we break it down, our emotions come from two sources: the unregenerated man, or the born again, Spirit-filled man. When the emotions come from the unregenerated part of man, they are carnal. They are opposite the Word of God and they want to be in control. Because the world does not understand Spirit-led living, they operate entirely by their emotions and intellect. To them it is fine to do whatever feels good. If they wake up in the morning and do not feel a positive emotion for their mate, they leave. It's no big deal. If they don't feel like showing up for work, they don't. Their life is in constant confusion because their emotions are always up and down. Up today, down tomorrow.

Let me tell you about an emotional roller coaster. I had an old beat-up Chevrolet truck. I loved my old truck, but I blew the engine in it. I parked it under a tree for four months thinking I'd put a new engine in it. I had another truck to drive, but I was going fix up my old truck. Up today-I'm going to put in a new engine. Next day, no, I'm going to sell it. Nope, I'm going to put in an engine. No, I'm going to sell it. This went on for months. Finally, I put a "for sale" sign on it and parked it by the side of the road. I put a pretty high price on it because I really didn't want to sell it, but it was a way to settle the emotional roller coaster. I'd put it out there for two days and then move it back into the barn for six days. My wife would ask about the truck, and I'd move it back out to the road. I wanted to settle those emotions. Up, down. Back, forth.

Finally, I decided I was going to fix the old truck and sell my new truck back to the dealer. I went home, and halfway through my meal-I hadn't even told my wife what I'd decided the phone rang. This gentleman said, "You told me if I wanted your truck I'd better get the money quick and come running. Well, I've got the money in my hand and I want to know if you can meet me right now." So I sold my old truck. When I went to bed that night, I didn't have to worry about that old truck any more.

The enemy will mess with your emotions. Sometimes when we go through valleys and tough times, we don't even realize we are under attack. People say you can't put a spiritual emphasis on every-thing that happens. The Bible says that the enemy is going to come immediately to steal, kill, destroy (John 10:10). As long as you're breathing, he will fight you. Did he not fight Christ every inch of the way? Why isn't he going to fight you then? We don't have to run scared. Greater is he that is in us, than he that is in the world (1 John 4:4). Neither do we have to second guess everything. We made a decision to marry, so let's stay married. Let's forget what it feels like.

Lots of people second guess God. They go to church on Sunday and say, "God is just what I need. God has really made a difference in my life. God has really helped me." They walk right out that door and fall into the valley of the shadow of death and the enemy says, "Where is your God now?" And they say, "I just don't think God can help me out of this one. God was okay last year. I remember thirty years ago he saved me, but times are hard and I just don't think God can help me right now." When the emotions begin to rule us, we get one thing-and it's not a headache, although that can happen too-we get confused. But our God is not the author of fear and confusion (1 Cor. 14:33).

Do you know what happens when we allow ourselves to be con-fused? We get distracted from the truth. It can even happen to churches. Remember, the church is not dead, the Word says it is to be alive (Rev. 3:1). If it is alive, it must have a soul. If it has a soul, it must have a will. If it has a will, it must have emotions. A church that is on an emotional roller coaster is confused and distracted. The church says one thing, but people see another.

Not too long ago, I told a minister friend of mine, "Sometimes I'm just the most miserable thing in the world. I should be the hap-piest of all. Look what God has worked through our lives. I should be thrilled, but I'm miserable."

He said, "What were you doing when you were happy?"

I thought about it and said, "It seems like I was in the top of that tree out on that little teeny tiny limb saying, 'Come on, God, let's go another mile.'"

My friend asked what happened. I said, "Well, I got back down to the bottom and started saying, 'I might fall down if I climb that tree.'"

He said, "Friend, you need to get your bottom end back up that tree and back out there on that limb. If that's where you were happy and that's where God called you to be, then get back up the tree. Get out on the limb. Do something besides sitting there and second guessing. Did He not say that He called you? Did God not say that He would equip you? Did He not say that the gifts and calling of God are without repentance? Are you not teaching the people that the devil hates their souls and he'll come after their will? He'll attack their emotions?"

"Yeah, yeah, I taught all that."

"Then why don't you live what you're teaching?"

Why is it so hard to live what we already know and do what we know is right? The flesh gets in the way. The devil likes to play games with us. The Bible says, "Behold thou desirest truth from the inward parts" (Ps. 51:6). That's from the heart. When we talk about these things, every one of us can pick out an area that we've been too emotional about. If you are an emotional person at home, then when you come into the body of believers, what are you going to be there? Emotional. What happens if there are twenty-five families that show up and fifteen or eighteen of them show up emotional? We're going to look like a crazy bunch of people who don't know what they're doing. All across America, God's people are guilty of having God's name warped because of this. A preacher stands up saying, "God gave me this," and thirty days later he's going through bankruptcy. God either gave it to you or He didn't. How can we know if He did or not? Don't say a word about it for ninety days. After that you can tell people what God did, and show them the proof.

A man once stood up on a Sunday night and testified that God had given him a well-paying welding job. The people clapped their hands and celebrated. It was a miracle. He hadn't had a job, and now he got hired to do a high-dollar job at the power plant. The next week he called me and said, "Remember what I said about that job? Well, the truth is that I had my interview today, and I didn't get the job. What am I going to do?" I wanted to tell him he needed to learn how to keep his mouth shut. Instead I tried to encourage him.

When you're on a high either from anger or happiness, come back down and find a balance and see how you feel about it. Be sure that it is God. When the enemy cannot gain entrance into our will, he will head for our emotions. Have you ever felt sorry for yourself? That is a sure sign that the enemy is going to mess up your mind. The greatest weapon you have that the enemy wants is your mind. If he can get you to believe that your spouse doesn't care or isn't faithful, and that the boss isn't treating you right, and this is not right and that's not right, he has you right where he wants you. Be careful.

When your emotions are acting up, the least little thing hurts your feelings. Why, that brother so-and-so didn't shake my hand. Well, when you think about it, brother so-and-so hasn't shaken your hand three times in six years, but all of a sudden because he didn't shake it Sunday there is something wrong. Or, I give my money in the offering but when I get out into the parking lot, I have a flat tire. Look what God did to me. Self pity.

I want you to be able to discern when the enemy is coming to attack you. Be careful with that emotional attack. During an attack, under fire, our first reaction is to withdraw for protection. When we withdraw, it pulls the harness off our emotions, allowing them to rule us. When self-pity becomes the basis from which we rule everything, the enemy is running havoc with us and our view becomes warped. We can't see straight for seeing crooked. I'm going to sell my truck. I'm going to keep my truck. I'm going to fix up my trailer. I'm going to sell my trailer. I'm going to give $50 in the offering. Nope, I'm going to give $20.

Because God allows people to choose for themselves what they are going to do, a lot of times, Monday, Tuesday, Wednesday He will lay on our hearts what we should do come Sunday. He'll allow you time to deal with your emotions to see if you are going to rationalize yourself right out of doing what He asked you to do.

We can rationalize our way out of doing what God called us to do. Every person could name at least five reasons why we should just sit and do nothing. But if we are going to stand true to God, somebody better get back up that tree. Somebody better get back out on that limb and somebody better say, "I don't care if I fall and skin my noggin, God will be there to wrap it up. I'm going to march on."

You can't shout victory just because you started with zero and in four years you've come to this place. You can't just say, "That's it, it's over. Look what we've done." You have to say, "Thank you, Lord, for winning that battle. Now help us win the next battle, and the next battle, and the next battle." We must not allow emotions to get the best of us.

The eyes of faith are gone when we are led by emotions, and are only moved by what we see in the natural. If we are only motivated by what we see in the natural, the devil will make sure we see and hear a lot.

One of the greatest steps toward emotional freedom is to get in the Book of Psalms. If anyone in the entire world ever had a right to be on an emotional roller coaster, it was David. He was anointed to be king and what was his first assignment? Tend sheep. He was right back where he started. How many times have we said, "God, I'm right back where I started." Just because He's going to start training you first, doesn't mean He didn't anoint you. Sometimes you have to be last before you can be first. Let me encourage you to get in the Book of Psalms. Before you read, say, "Lord, I'm reading Psalms because I want you to help my emotions." David was always crying out and singing a song because he was fighting his emotions. Let the Book of Psalms be an encouragement to you.

CHAPTER THIRTEEN

INTELLIGENCE UNDER FIRE

The enemy wants you to withdraw from others so he can begin to tear your faith down. If he can get you alone, he can work on T you individually. It's a lot harder for him to rend a group than it is for him to tear one of us apart. There is strength in unity, together-ness, oneness. There is great power when a group comes together in one mind and one accord. Then the power of the Holy Spirit comes.

The Anger Connection

The enemy also comes against our emotions through anger, especially when we've been hurt by someone. Why is it always another believer who hurts you and not the world? It is because the enemy is trying to get brothers and sisters against each other so that they have no faith in God's word. When you dwell on that hurt, you get angry. And after you get angry, you get anxious. You get to the place where the only satisfaction you get is when you see your brother hurting. There is a verse in Romans that says "if you pray for your enemy, it heaps hot coals of fire upon his head" (Romans 12:20). I used to think that prayer was my $20 front row seat to watch God take care of them. But God will never, ever take care of someone else the way we think He will. It took me a long time to learn that. In fact, I got mad at God a few times. I said,

"Listen, Lord, if you're not going to take care of them, I guarantee I can take care of them."

When self-pity and anger show up, you know your emotions are being attacked. Now we need to know what to do about it. I like the things David said. In Psalms, from chapter one all the way to the very last chapter, he says things like:

"Oh Lord, open thou my lips and my mouth shall show forth thy praise" (51:15).

- "Make me to hear joy and gladness" (51:8).
- "I trust in the mercy of God for ever and ever" (52:8).
- "I will hear what God the Lord will speak, for He will speak the peace of His people" (85:8).
- "Why art thou cast down, oh my soul, and why art thou disquieted within me?" (42:11).
- "Hope thou in God, for I shall yet praise Him who is the health of my countenance" (42:5).

All through the Book of Psalms, David is crying out to the Lord. It's an outcome against that emotional attack. Sometimes we just need to get into Psalms and say, "Lord, I need strength. I need you to put to rest this battle I'm having to face." Psalms will lift you up, give you a song, and help you. "Lord, how long?" David cried. "How long will I go through this? How long will I face adversity?" (Ps. 13:1-2, paraphrased). David was spiritually taking control of his emotions. You can have all the pity parties, but until you get into the Word and let the Word take control, you can't come against those emotional attacks.

Extraordinary Intelligence

Once we've dealt with the emotional state, we need to deal with the intellect. The human brain is extraordinary. No scientist or medical doctor is able to explain how a small mass of tissue can retain and understand knowledge. Human intelligence is unexplainable to science because God created it to function in His image. God intended the intellect of man to function in His image, not according to the image of the world. But human intelligence in the wrong vein can be a work against God. Someone told me not long ago, "I know what I know and you're not going to change me." There are a lot of areas in which I feel I'm right, but God is always showing me that He is righter.

In the world, intelligence places humans in class categories. It does not see all men as equal. One of the greatest tragedies in the church world is that people expect everyone to look, act, and sing alike. If we all had to sit in the same seat, there would be a big fight come Sunday morning. We are made to be different, but the mentality of the world is to judge.

We spend all of our time judging each other and God said He was the judge. When David was being chosen as king, Samuel looked at David's brother, who was muscular, trim, and fit and said, "Now he would make a good king." But God said, "Hold it. You're looking at man's outward appearance, but I look at the heart of man" (1 Sam. 16:6-7 paraphrased). God looks at the inside, and sees the intelligent part of the heart. The intellect of the world is so different, and sadly, the church is too busy trying to be just like the world.

The intellect of A person is to fit into the image of God, not to fit into the ways of the world. It's like saying, "I'm going to live as close as I can to God, but I'm also going to stay just as far as I can into the world. I want the best of both worlds." The Word talks about straddling the fence in Luke 16:13. You have to be one or the other. Intelligence was placed inside man to help him understand the workings of God and cause prosperity to abound in the earth. Mixed with the Spirit of God, intelligence accomplishes great feats. No matter what culture we are in, if we prosper in that environment, intelligence serves us. For a long time I thought I was going to preach like a certain preacher, only to find that wasn't me. Once, when I was trying to get into the intensive care ward to visit someone who had open heart surgery, I told the nurse I was a pastor and she said, "You don't look like no pastor." I know who I am, and I know what I am, and I know what God called me to be.

As soon as we give in to the opinions of people, we have taken our first step toward failure. Pretty soon we want to please men, so we start trying to fit that mold. I preached a certain way for quite some time, hoping I was pleasing some people, only to have eight families get up and walk out. I had to go home and be whipped spiritually because I had been trying to fit in. We must learn to be what God called us to be.

Godly Intelligence

For the believer, intelligence works with our spirit to cause understanding. God desires to reveal Himself to us, and to have us know His ways. Isaiah 1:18 says, "Come now, and let us reason together, saith the LORD: though your sins be as scarlet, they shall be as white as snow; though they be red like crimson, they shall be as wool." God delights in using our intelligence to show us His ways. The Hebrew interpretation for the word reason in this Scripture means to decide or convict. Our intelligence has a part to play in conviction and in submission to God. The Bible says in Psalms 14:1 that only a fool would say there is no God. Proverbs 19:8 says, "He that getteth wisdom loveth his own soul."

It's the intellect that decides to dig into the Word and see what we are supposed to be. Have you ever doubted God? I have. There have been times when God was God enough for me, and there have been other times when I've said, "God, you're not enough. This problem is too big. Lord, you brought me out into the wilderness and left me." That's the enemy coming against the intellect, to weaken your mind and spirit so you begin to question the things of God. Only a fool would say there Is no God.

Intelligence will turn into Godly wisdom only if we mature our souls according to the Word. If I'm walking through the valley of the shadow of death, I need to ask the Lord what this means. Why am I going through this valley? Why am I walking through this pain? Why is my spirit so disturbed? He will begin to speak to me spiritually. He will give me understanding. He will cause the intellect to rise up and understand that this thing is of God and that God is using it to mature my soul and make me stronger. You get stronger in the Lord by going through the valley. I can't say that I like it, but I've gained much more strength in the valley than I have on the mountain top. Think about the last time you were on the mountain. How much and how often did you pray and fast and read the Word? Think about the last time you were in the valley. Now how often did you pray and fast? Every day. God has to keep some folks in the valley. A marriage can never be prosperous until the partners have learned what marriage stands for. A church can never be a true church until we have sought the wisdom of God. Proverbs 2:7 says, "He layeth up sound wisdom for the righteous," and Proverbs 3:13 says, "Happy is the man that findeth wisdom."

Natural Intelligence

Godly intelligence produces peace and security, but natural intelligence resists God because it wants to rule in God's place. Natural intelligence thinks that it is wiser than God and it sets up rules and regulations to prove it. Natural intelligence tries to figure everything out. I've come across people who love to get into books and research and always want to dissect things. I don't care how you prove it by the Word, they disregard anything supernatural because they cannot comprehend it in their natural mind.

If you are always in your natural mind-trying to figure out God, you'll never figure Him out. It will never make sense that you can push somebody into church in a wheelchair and they can walk out later. Scientists can't prove it, so they dissect it.

You need to be careful who and what you believe in. If you always have to justify the Scripture, then something is wrong, because God makes it plain. People of the natural intellect rationalize that there are no miracles. The Gospels aren't logical, they say. The Bible gave us the Pharisees and Sadducees as good examples of intelligent men who reasoned their service to God into works alone. There was no worship and service from the heart; they were just doing things for the Lord.

We can't follow the leading of the Spirit if we are always in the natural mind. In my natural mind, I know I need to mow the lawn this week. In my natural mind, I know I have to be sure my children are up and ready for the bus in the morning. We can accomplish a lot of things in the natural, but we can't live in the natural. We have to get into the Spirit and say, "Lord, I don't just want to get the kids on the bus today, I want to have meaning." The spiritual is what gives meaning.

Intellectual Attacks

Remember that no matter what you are facing, it is the goal of the enemy to dethrone God from His rightful position in your life. How can you tell when your intelligence is being attacked? First and foremost, logic overrides the inward witness. The inward witness says it's going to be okay, that God is building your faith. The inward witness says that you may be weeping tonight, but there will be joy in the morning. The natural says, "You've done it this time. You're not going to make it through this month. Your marriage will never stand another week of this. You've ruined your children." See the difference?

There comes a time when we have to look at what God is in us and not what man thinks God is in us. We must be careful. We take a God who knows and sees everything, and who is working out His plan in our lives, and tear down what He is trying to do and put it into the natural. We say, "I could worship if they'd turn the pews just a little more." Or, "If it wasn't so cool in here, and if the air conditioner didn't make so much noise, I could worship." The enemy will do anything he can to keep us off base.

Intelligence is very important to God. Godly intellect causes us to respond in the image of God, not in the likeness of men. We can't go out and paint the church just because somebody says they believe they could feel God if there was a hit of blue on the walls. We can't live like that. We must understand that the enemy hates us and is coming after our souls. Maybe he's failed to get to you in other ways, so now he's trying to make you feel you're not good enough. He did it to Moses, didn't he? God said to Moses, "I've equipped you." Moses threw out all of his natural intellectual questions and God gave him all the right answers. In the end, God just got frustrated with Moses. The anger of the Lord was kindled against him" (Exod. 4:14). Don't you think the anger of the Lord ever gets kindled against His people for their shallowness? Ask the Lord to keep you from being a person who has all the answers when you don't even know all the questions. When these things happen, before long you feel cold and dead inside. You don't pray. Or you pray with a sarcastic heart. You don't believe God for miracles any longer, and you certainly will not tolerate the preaching of the Word. You become just like a wounded animal out in the field, with a buzzard circling overhead. When that animal goes down and can't protect itself, the buzzard goes in for the kill. It is the same thing spiritually.

We are smart people, because God gave us an intelligence comparable to His. When we act out of ignorance, we are in essence saying, "God, I don't want you. What you offered and what you gave me is not good enough. I'm better than that."

If the devil cannot get you to question the existence of God, then he will try to throw you over into the road of no common sense. I heard a preacher ask why it is that when some people are born again, they seem to throw out their common sense. Have you ever wondered that? God expects us to use common sense. If you stick your finger on the hot burner, you will get burned. "But I'm living by faith, you say. No, you're living by ignorance. If you step out in front of a speeding bullet, faith is not going to do you a bit of good. There are those who confess healing scriptures all day but go outside in sub-zero weather without a coat. They don't take care of their bodies but they expect the blessings of God in the area of healing. God is not going to bless you for being ignorant. That's why He gave you intelligence. If you go outside with-out a coat in sub-zero weather, you deserve what you get.

Then there are those who constantly speak prosperity on themselves and others, but never look for a job. There are also those with families who assume each member of that family knows how much they love them. They never take time to say, "I love you, I care about you, and I appreciate you." I've noticed with my children that if I don't take time out to tell them just how special they are, they seem to with-draw from me. Everybody likes to be stroked now and then. Sometimes we get so intelligent and high and mighty, we forget to tell those we are closest how special they are.

It is not God's will for us to be an ignorant people. We must not be deceived in the area of common sense and we cannot take the important details for granted. Do not look at the Word of God as a cure-all if you have not done your part. The Bible says when you have done all that you can do, stand (Eph. 6:136). Some of us got into some messes in our lives over a period of time; it didn't just happen. We owe it to God to give Him time to change us and work it out. That's why the Bible speaks of sanctification. When you are saved, the seed of sanctification has been planted. The Lord sanctifies us day by day. It's a process.

So how do we recover when our intellect is under attack? If you know you have allowed your natural intellect to be used for some-thing other than what God would have it, repent. You must come to a place where you say, "Lord, I'm so sorry. I see that the enemy has been messing with me. God, you didn't make me an ignorant person, but I haven't been acting the way I should." And then you rebuke that foul spirit, saying, "You just get off me. I'm God's chosen. He gave me intelligence so my life would reflect the image of God."

Psalms 119:63 says, "I am a companion of all them that fear thee, and of them that keep thy precepts." Psalms 111:10 says, "The fear of the LORD is the beginning of wisdom: a good understanding have all they that do His commandments." If you've been attacked, get around some believers and start gaining strength from them. You can only stand so high and so strong on your own two feet. You need God to conquer. Allow Him to change your way of thinking and give you strength.

CHAPTER FOURTEEN

THE IMAGINATION

I have quite an imagination. Sometimes when I share something I've imagined with my wife, she'll say, "Oh, mercy," because she knows what I do with my imagination. Sometime back I drove around behind a motel and saw about fifty toilets sitting there. They looked like good ones to me. My imagination just ran wild. My wife said, "Oh, no. Sanford and Son, here we go." We hauled those toilets home, sold them and put the money into our new church building. I'll sell another truck load of them if I can get my hands on any more.

The human imagination is a part of our soul, yet vastly different from the other parts. We have the ability to imagine beyond our intelligence. Five and a half years ago I began to pray, "Lord, I know it is your will for my family to be involved in starting a new work, but I can't just give it a simple name. Something tells me that I need to be different." It is okay to be different. You may not have a lot of friends being different, but it's okay to be different. God didn't send me here to make friends. He sent me here to share the good news that Jesus can save souls from the devil's hell. Jesus will pick you up, heal your broken heart, mend your puzzled mind, draw your imagination back into His spiritual realm, and make you what He wants you to be. I said, "Lord I can't just name it Summerfield Church of God." While walking around the neighborhood one day, with my spiritual eyes I saw common folks in a surgical ward, wearing intensive care uniforms, ministering to people. One was strung out on drugs; another was in a wheelchair. Someone had their spiritual arms blown off. Another came from a broken home. I asked God what it meant and He said," Intensive Care." What an imagination. I was scared to use the name "Intensive Care," so we started as "Summerfield Church of God." About six months into it, I couldn't take it any longer, and we became "Intensive Care."

Glorified Imagination

God uses the imagination for His glory. You can imagine some-thing and still not put it together intelligently. We might envision a goal or a dream and still not know how to get there. Our imagination has the creative ability to do anything for God. There are many, many, visions from God that have been placed on the shelf because we don't believe in our imaginations. We haven't allowed things to get out of the natural and into the spiritual.

If my wife cooked a bad meal, I could dwell on that bad meal and it would ruin the rest of my day. Or I could say she just had a bad day, no big deal, let's go on. It's the imagination. Have you noticed that when things are shaky at home, they always look better across the fence? When your vehicle is just a little dirty, instead of going out and washing it, you look over at your neighbor's new car.

When we do not understand the principle of imagination, we will dream our lives away. Faith is not fantasy. Idle imaginations can-not pro-duce anything-physically or spiritually. Imagination without action and its accurate timing is fruitless. Sometimes God allows us to see things, but that's just the first step toward God using us. Then we have to seek God for the timing. Have you ever been out of tim-ing with God? I've been out of timing a few times. I said some things I wish I hadn't, and later realized I was just a little out of time. We have to have the spirit of discernment to know what is happening so we don't jump time.

It is our place to discern what is of God and what is not. When you begin to see how God works, it is an awesome place to be. It's an awe-some walk when God continuously lets you see things. People some-times ask what keeps me going. I see something out there a call from God, a light from heaven-and all I have to do is stay on the straight and narrow. God begins to work through the imagination and the spirit man. He begins to show you things. If people would get on their faces and seek God, He would give them that same vision. "God help me dis-cern what in my imagination is of you, and what is in there that has nothing to do with you."

The imagination will just run wild with the things of God. It will run wild with you. Have you ever had an inner feeling, but thought, "No, people will laugh at me. They just won't receive that." An imagination without works is a dead, useless dream. If God gives you a spiritual dream to go and minister to someone, the occasion will not always be there. When He speaks to you, there is a reason that He speaks it at that time. He expects you to put legs on that dream, that vision, that imagination, and move ahead. He didn't call us to the middle of the desert and say, "Okay, you are on your own." Why did the children of Israel spend a long time in the desert?

Disobedience? Rebellion? Always wanting to know everything? Why Did it take them so long to get where they needed to go? At one point God was so frustrated with them, he said "I'm going to wipe them out."

Did Moses say "Thank God. I'll be glad for you to take this burden off me?" No. Moses said "Lord, you can't do that. Our enemies are going to know that you brought your people out here and destroyed them." See, there was an imagination for the people to be set free and someone went to answer the call. But the people had to know everything. You don't always have to know everything.

The imagination is a powerful force. God is a spirit, and they who worship God must worship God in spirit and in truth (John 4:24). That tells me something has to happen internally for me to communicate. My spirit and His Spirit must somehow connect. How are we to connect if He can't speak to me? When He tells me He wants me to plan a new ministry, how can I know which way to go if He doesn't plant the seed in my imagination how I can accomplish it? He doesn't tell me to buy a bag of 16-penny nails and a whole box of 10-penny nails; He leaves that up to me. God is God. What matters is that I worship him in spirit and in truth. What matters is that with every step I take, I have to be sure that I move one step closer to Him.

Have you ever had to walk through a briar patch? Sometimes I feel like I can't get out of the briar patch. But as long as I know that God is in there somewhere, I'm going to keep on tromping. There are some good old blackberries in the briar patch, too.

Imagination is very important to God. If you can imagine it, it is within your reach. For many years I thought I was a weirdo because I was always thinking up crazy stuff. I'm just beginning to figure out I'm normal. God said His people was a peculiar people (1 Pet. 2:9). You're not going to think like the average, everyday person. You might as well quit trying to find friends outside the Kingdom of God. Make up your mind that if you're going to serve God and imagine the things of God, then you're going to have relationships inside the Kingdom. God has imagined something for my life and it has helped me imagine some things for God. It's amazing how it works.

Selfish Imagination

A selfish imagination is always about me, me, me. With a selfish Imagination, I'm always down on you. People complain that we could do better in the church if others would give more money. That's not the problem. We would do better in the church if we could be satisfied with what people do give. Thank God someone gave a penny. My cup may be half empty, but praise God, it's half full. It's in the way I see it.

With a selfish imagination, you can't accomplish anything for God. Can I tell you what turned our marriage around? I quit being selfish, and she quit being selfish. I beat my feet a little harder at the front door to get the dirt off, and she yelled at me a little bit less for holding the door open and letting the flies in. I don't mind biscuits with flies on them, but she can't stand it. So we had to come together on this thing. Imagination can make or break you. Look at the imagination of David. In Genesis 11:6a the Lord said, "behold the people are one." I could camp here a while. God's people are going to have to get on the same page. It doesn't matter if you are Baptist or Catholic or Presbyterian; we are God's people. He gave the same son on the same cross for you and for me. It doesn't matter from what side of the tracks we come. The Lord said the people are one, and they all have one language. They were either all griping or all praising. They were either all imagining God to be something really awesome, or they were imagining God to be something really small. We can be all in the same vein; the question is, in what vein?

How do you see yourself? Do you feel deep down in your heart that you have a particular calling? On the day of Pentecost, they were all in one mind and all had one language. They all were dreaming, but I don't think they imagined the power of God coming the way it did. That's the joy of serving God. We don't know how He is going to work.

I walked across our field one day just a ball of nerves. I found myself mumbling and grumbling and griping. I got to the other side and started sharing with a gentleman about some of the things God had done. By the time I got back across the field, I was ready to have church, because my imagination had been struck. God said, "Son, don't you remember the good things? You haven't seen anything yet." My imagination is coming together and regrouping and I'm seeing so many things, I don't know which way to go with them.

"And the LORD said, Behold, the people is one, and they have all one language; and this they begin to do: and now nothing will be restrained from them, which they have imagined to do" (Gen. 11:6). We know that the tower of Babel was not a good idea, but even in rebellion, the principle of unity worked.

I was really excited about something recently and told my wife it felt like the first time I saw her twenty years ago. I walked into a Pizza Inn, saw her waiting on tables and thought, "My, my, my." I said to some church friends, "Do you see her? I'm going to ask her out, and then I'm going to marry her." They called her over and said, "You see that tall drink of water over there? He says he's going to marry you." Back then my hair was all streaked down and I weighed 128 pounds soaking wet. She said, "That nut is not taking me anywhere." Guess what? I imagined; I took her out; and I married her.

If we, by God's Spirit, can imagine that every need will be met, then they will be met. If we can imagine that, by His Spirit, He has walked into the room, He can heal our bodies, save our souls, lift our hope, and fill our pockets. He says, "Everything that they imagined was conquered." Where's your faith? If you're hurting, my God will heal you.

Have you ever rationalized your way right out of a miracle? I have, and I had to go home and say, "Man, you are just dumb." Most of the time when I'm telling myself I'm dumb, it's because I get so down. The enemy has come against this imagination God gave me. Look at David. David's brothers were out there murmuring and complaining about who was going to kill the giant. Nobody was going to kill that giant. And little old David imagined what was going to happen to the head of that giant. He didn't walk up and say, "Let me kill the giant." No, he said, "Is there not a cause, is there not a reason to fight, is there not a reason to shout?" (1 Sam. 17:29 paraphrased). They said, "The armor doesn't even fit you." He said, "Just put me in something and let me go. I'll show you what fits" (17:39, paraphrased).

If many moons ago you imagined you and a particular person together, and you made a commitment to be together, then be together. Have I ever had an opportune time in nineteen years to walk out? You bet. But I can't let go of what God gave me. The devil says, "Man, you've done all you can do here. Just pack your bags." I'm not packing my bags. I cut the backs out of all my suitcases. Some of us need to unpack and say "God, here I am. I have a need. I'm suffering in my body, I've lost my hope, I need direction."

If we can imagine what God can do in our lives! He said there is not one thing that is out of reach. I've come to a place in my life where there is no better friend than Jesus. Oh, that's my song. He's my Jesus. In the midnight hour when no one can understand and no one can get there, He's my friend.

If you need a touch from the Lord, the Lord will touch you. He will heal your finances. He will pick you up when you are down on your luck and He'll give you hope. The things that He has allowed you to imagine, He'll bring real life to them. It's not his will for you to go through life all turned upside down. That's not His will.

Learn how to survive what the enemy meant for destruction. Take control of your imagination. Whatever your need is, start by giving praise. Imagine that back healed. Imagine that new engine in the pick-up truck. Imagine…and praise.

CHAPTER FIFTEEN

REALITY CHECK

What constitutes a godly imagination? It's simple: reality or unreality. When you are right with God, He will not give you a vision, a dream, or an imagination that is off in left field. He won't tell you to tear your home apart and say it's all in the name of God. Neither will He tell you to harm your family and cause them to suffer. There are a lot of people with a warped imagination. A Godly imagination is an imagination of reality.

Many have been buffaloed in their lifetime. The enemy has come in and messed with them and sometimes overtaken them before they recognized it. But we're not going to be ignorant. Anytime grass on the other side of the fence is looking greener, that's unreality. You can't have what is there. If whatever is there is looking greener, try watering your own grass. Clean up and fix up what is yours. That is reality.

Reality is not being envious of what someone else has. The enemy will try to get us to imagine crazy things. It would be foolish of me to say our new church building will be paid for by the time we step through the door. I believe with all my heart this project will be 100% paid for, though it may take us fifteen years to get there. That's reality.

Reality is believing God will heal me, but He may not choose to do so. He may choose to work whatever ails me as a blessing so He can receive glory. I appreciate the pews in our church because they are soft and look nice. But I don't appreciate them nearly as much as the four or five men who moved them. I didn't get any blisters for that blessing.

Fighting Fantasy

Tune in on any television program and you see fantasy. You see fantasy on 85% or 90% of the billboards in America. Is it reality to be smoking a Marlboro cigarette, you in a fine looking cowboy hat while riding a million dollar horse? That's not going to happen. I imagined when I was fifteen years old that by the time I was twenty-six, I was going to retire. That was not reality.

Lucifer imagined that he was going to rise above the most High. There are devils in people who imagine tearing apart what God is trying to build. But if we are a people of reality by God's Spirit, the moment they walk in we'll say, "Uh-uh, won't happen here." It matters what is being played on your television at home. It is important to know who your children are hanging out with. It's not that I don't trust my daughter to be on the phone at 10 or 11 o'clock at night, I just want to know what they're talking about.

The reality is that there is always someone trying to destroy and tear apart what God has given me. The enemy has imagined that he can tear down the children of God. He'd love to tear my life down. The enemy has an imagination too, and he takes the power of that imagination and tries to push us overboard. He wants things to be a fantasy to us, a fairy tale. I can drive up and down the road and imagine having a different woman, but the reality is that when I get home tonight, the wife who's been there for Forty five years will be there. That's reality.

The Word doesn't say run and see that I'm God. No, it says, "Stand there. Be still. Know that I am God" (Ps. 46:10 paraphrase). Lucifer thought he was going to rise above God. He had it all planned out, even had a few who were going to rise with him, but Christ said He saw him fall from heaven like lightning (Luke 10:18).

In Genesis 3:4-5, Satan used the principle of imagination on Eve. He showed her the fruit and caused her to imagine its taste and texture. Now God had said, "Keep your hands off it." But the enemy came and said, "You won't believe how good the fruit tastes. I'll tell you why God doesn't want you to eat of it; because you'll know whatever he knows. You'll be like God and that's why that selfish God is holding it back from you." The enemy just steadily talked to Eve. What else did He say? "Ye shall not surely die: For God doth know that in the day ye eat thereof, then your eyes shall be opened, and ye shall be as gods, know-ing good and evil" (Gen. 3:4b-5). Eve took her husband and they went and grabbed a piece of fruit (Gen. 3:6).

If you're going to give in to temptation and to the wiles and the attacks of the enemy, go by yourself. I tell my children, "If you're in an automobile and the driver gets out and steals a piece of bubble gum, you're all guilty."

While my brother and I were growing up, I don't know who had more whippings, him or me. But I never took a whooping for him. And he never stepped up and said, "Daddy whip me instead of Donnie." Uh-uh. It just wasn't that way. He got himself in trouble and he had to deal with it. When I got myself in trouble, I had to deal with my trouble.

2 Corinthians 10:5 says, "Casting down imaginations, and every high thing that exalteth itself against the knowledge of God." How many times have we said, "I lay my bondage on the altar tonight," and then got up and picked up that heavy load and taken it back home with us? The enemy can warp your imagination. The word says to cast down imaginations and every high thing that exalteth itself against the knowledge of God. Your family was supposed to be home at 3:00, and now it's 4:00 and you begin to imagine everything possible. They ran off a cliff; the car blew up; they had a head-on collision; they've been kidnapped; they're dead. That kind of imagining brings fear and confuses what you know to be true. I know we should care and be concerned, but we don't have to live in fear. God is faithful and just until the end, so I'm not going to live in fear.

The second part of 2 Corinthians 10:5 says, "...and bringing into captivity every thought to the obedience of Christ." So here we are, living our lives, working at our jobs, raising our children, trying to be the best husband or wife we can be, cutting the lawn, making sure food's on the table, keeping the vehicles running. Then all of a sudden, things begin to turn sour. Much worse than a bad hair day, we go through some unpleasant times. We immediately blame God. He's my savior, but I can't believe He did that to me.

The Scripture says to bring all those foolish thoughts into captivity. Bring them into the obedience of God's Word. The Scripture in a really nice, gentle way of saying "Shut up. Stop it. Quit thinking those crazy thoughts."

Imaginations that exalt themselves over the Word of God are not from heaven. It is vitally important that you pay attention to what you are imagining. God has begun to deal with my imagination. He's helping me understand I am working for Him, not man. And He has helped me to imagine the things that are of God and not the things that are of man.

If you're going to do something spectacular for the kingdom's sake, you're going to have to learn to control your thoughts. You must be able to discern what is reality and what is unreality. When you dream it and think it and know in your heart it's God, sit on it for a few days, contemplate it, and see if it is feasible. God never calls us to a particular calling without equipping us.

CHAPTER SIXTEEN

MEMORY MADNESS

Have you ever asked your child, "Why did you do that?" The answer you got was "I don't know."

"Where did you get that from?"

"I don't know."

"Who told you that?"

"I don't know." They may good and well have the right answer, but they say they don't know. Memory is a very powerful part of the soul. Our soul is not just will, emotion, intellect, and imagination, it also includes memory. Memory has the power to make or break you. Have you ever headed down the highway and forgot where you were going? Your memory left you. Memory has the power to store what someone says, what you see, hear, say, read. Memory stores everything Think back to things you can remember from your earliest childhood. Memory is amazing.

I can recall a day when I was out on a piece of equipment and suddenly, I forgot where I was. I forgot who I was. Fear gripped me and chills ran up and down my spine. The Spirit of the Lord said, "Son everything's going to be okay." When I heard that voice in my spirit, immediately my mind came back. I knew where I was, I knew how I had gotten there, and I knew what I was supposed to be doing. It is a fearful thing when one loses his mind or memory.

Sometimes the spirit of the Lord shares some things with me and I'll think, "I've got to remember that." But by the time I get to the office or to a place where I can write it down, I have to say, "Lord could you repeat that one more time?" I've already heard something in the house of the Lord I wanted to apply in my life, but before I got out to my car, I'd even forgotten what the preacher preached. See how the enemy steals?

Stolen Memory

The enemy steals away in our marriages too. Just a few years ago you were madly in love, but all of a sudden you don't know this person you're living with, so how can you love her? That's the enemy taking away. He comes to steal, kill, destroy.

I don't want my memory to escape me. When I read Scripture, I'm praying, "Lord, help me remember." I want to take what God has for me, and I want to remember it. I want God to clear my mind and make room. I have to go into my computer sometimes and clear out the trash-things I saved that I don't really need. Some of us are bound because we remember too much of the past. We can't move ahead with peace and joy because we are so tied by what's behind us. You can choose how you use your memory, You can either remember the bad things that bring depression, hurt, and more pain, or you can remember the good things of God. You say you've never had a valley quite like this one. You never had a valley like the last one either, but God brought you through it. If He brought you through that one, He'll bring you through this one.

Sometimes we have to rely on our memory to encourage us. I know of a ministry where, if you need counseling, they schedule you three months out for an appointment with the pastor. The criteria for having that appointment is you can't miss any Sunday morning, Sunday night, or Wednesday night service. If you miss one service, you start all over again for three months. If, after three months of Bible study, Sunday school, ministry time and worship, you still need counseling, they'll counsel you. They usually counsel one person out of a hundred. Ninety percent of the time, all we need to do is remember from where God brought us. Remember who Christ is. Remember what He accomplished. He said He bore the stripes for everything. Every issue that we would ever deal with, Christ walked through. He conquered when He died. Therefore we should be dead to the things that come against us. But we forget.

Isn't it a shame that Christians have to spend so much time persuading other believers that they can make it, that it's okay to move ahead, and that God is still alive and on the throne. Think how much time we waste. My wife and I have decided not to waste each other's time. She doesn't ask me what she should cook for dinner, and I don't ask her which lawn mower or gas can to use. There comes a time when believers have to remember what God is doing. To stay with what God is doing, you have to keep moving. You can't just sit there and say, "I'll catch Him on the next time." He may not come back around.

Take It Back

In 1 Samuel 17:33 it says, "Saul said to David, Thou art not able to go against this Philistine to fight with him: for thou art but a youth, and he is a man of war from his youth." That would be enough to scare off most of us.

David's response was, "Thy servant kept his father's sheep, and there came a lion, and a bear, and took a lamb out of the flock: And I went out after him, and smote him, and delivered it out of his mouth: and when he arose against me, I caught him by his beard, and smote him, and slew him" (1 Sam. 17:34-35). David said he not only chased him down and stopped him from having a party with his goods, but he took it from him. As Christians, we are bold enough to stand up and rebuke the enemy, but are we bold enough to take back what is ours? If you lost your peace, go take it back. Remember the times God delivered you, because if He delivered you then, He's going to deliver you again. People argue that we can't be bold with God. I believe God would much rather hear us say, "Lord, I'm going to remind you of your Word. If you conquered the enemy for David, you can conquer my enemy. God, I'm going to put you to the test. I'm going to take back what belongs to me." You're not going to hurt God's feelings unless you reject him. Some years ago a young man packed his suitcase just before a Sunday night service and said, "I'm going to go to the house of the Lord, and I'm not going home until I receive the Holy Ghost." Sometimes we just have to have a made up mind.

"Thy servant slew both the lion and the bear: and this uncircumcised Philistine shall be as one of them, seeing he hath defied the armies of the living God" (1 Sam. 17:36). David told Saul he was going to respond to this enemy exactly the way he responded to the other enemy. The enemy is the enemy is the enemy… David's memory reminded him and gave him strength. He said, "Is there not a cause?" (1 Sam. 17:29). He's saying, "Good grief, guys, look who we serve. Look who the Father is." Sometimes we have to come in and say, "Hey wake up! God's on the throne!"

David said, "Moreover, The LORD that delivered me out of the paw of the lion, and out of the paw of the bear, he will deliver me out of the hand of this Philistine. And Saul said unto David, Go, and the LORD be with thee" (1 Sam. 17:37). Saul realized he may as well leave David alone, because David's mind was made up. David relied on the power of his memory to give him the strength to go out and defeat the enemy. He knew what God had done in the past. Think how much courage we could gain if we remembered the experiences we've had with God, and if we shared with others where the Father has led us.

Fifty six years ago, I was confined in a Lake City, Florida hospital. The doctors told my parents there was no hope. "Your son has leukemia." I remember walking out to a little fruit stand across the street from the hospital with my parents to get a chocolate drink. Just from the sun and the heat, my nose poured blood. I'll never forget it. I also remember the nurse who would come in every day, strap me down, and give me shots in places I didn't enjoy. I think back to where I've walked for the last thirty-one years. I recall a time as a teeth-ager, my mother caught me doing some things she hadn't raised us to do. She found a pack of cigarettes under my bed, and by all practical rea soning, she should have whooped me. But I'll never forget the greatest whooping I ever had from her. She looked at me just as serious and loving as a mother could, and said, "Son, why do you want to do that to your body when you know Jesus healed you and gave you another chance at life? You really disappoint me." Then she walked out of that room. Times when I've been tempted to do the wrong thing, my memory reminds me from where God brought me.

There is a reason I'm here. It wasn't a mistake. It wasn't some fairy tale. It's not a mistake for you to be right where you are at this moment. The experiences that you've had, those valleys, have not been a mistake. God has allowed you to walk through the low places so you could help someone else. It's such a blessing when you find others who are walking through what you've been delivered of, and you can say, "There are a lot of things 1 don't know, but let me tell you what I do know. Be gentle. We don't want to kick someone when they're down. I've had people give a testimony and really hurt me with it. We need to learn how to pick people up. Ask God to give you wisdom. He'll speak through you. You can be Spirit led, like David. He remembered where God brought him from, and what a mighty God and what a mighty fortress He is. David remembered that if he was victorious one time, he would be victorious again. His memory served him well.

In 2 Timothy 4:17, Paul said something similar. "Not with standing the Lord stood with me and strengthened me." The Lord didn't leave him or forsake him. He had gone through troubled times, and he was facing troubled times again. It was two-fold, just like for the believer. Paul said, "The Lord stood with me. He was right by my side just like He said He would be. And not only was He with me..."

I have seen people so bound by burdens and brokenness that someone had to hold them upright so they could stand for prayer. That is what Christ does for us on a daily basis. He is forever standing there. He is our strength, our comfort, and our guide. He was my strength yesterday. He is my strength today. And He is going to be my strength tomorrow.

Paul was saying that no matter what I have to face, God's going to be there. No matter how deep the valley, no matter how badly I hurt, no matter how many friends I lose, God's going to be there. Just to prove that he believed what he was saying, he adds, "To God be the glory forever and forever and forever and forever." It is time to stop moaning and groaning, griping and grumbling, and start praising.

Courage for the Task

Paul also relied on the power of his memory to give him courage to fulfill his mission on earth. He remembered that if God delivered him from evil before, He would do it again. He said to Timothy, "Wherefore I put thee in remembrance" (2 Tim. 1:6a). Remembrance is digging into your memory. God saved you out of a life of sin. You were a lost sinner without hope, happiness, peace, or joy. And then one day, because you prayed and asked Him to, Christ came into your heart and forgave you. Stir up and renew your salvation.

Have you ever had God speak to you, and you knew that it was God? Stir up that Word. People tell me the Lord used to speak to them all the time, but they haven't heard Him say anything lately. They quit listening, because He's always talking. Sometimes so many things start running through my mind, I feel like I'll go crazy before I get it all on paper.

Paul said, "For God hath not given us the spirit of fear; but of power, and of love, and of a sound mind" (2 Tim. 1:7). If we stir up our memory for God, we will move in faith, not fear. It is a disgrace to the Father in heaven when a believer lives in fear. We can't respond in ignorance, and we have to take precautions when there is a storm coming, but we don't have to live in fear.

As a believer, you must put faith in the words you speak. When you bless God out of one side of your mouth and curse him out of the other, people don't understand and it breeds confusion. The saddest moment in a Christian's life is when an unbeliever looks at them and says, "I don't see anything different in your life." Lord, help my memory to be what it should be. I don't want to live in fear. I want to live in faith.

If the enemy can harass and torment your memory, he will paralyzed you. A while back I asked my wife not to bring me the whole month's worth of bills on the first day of the month. Seeing that whole stack can paralyze me with fear. But, I have learned to handle it a week at a time. Something else may paralyze you with fear. Calm down and say, "Lord, I'm going to learn to trust you day-by-day, instead of month-by-month."

Too many of us make a mess out of our lives and then expect God to straighten it all out in one trip to the altar "Lord, you see the mess I made in 40 years. I'm giving you 15 seconds to straighten it out, and if you can't do it, you're not for real." God just may say, "Okay, I'm not for real," because He wants us to live by faith. We live by faith by what goes on in our memory. When I remember where He's brought me from and what He has already worked in my life, it strengthens me and then fear leaves.

If the enemy can take hurts and store them in your memory to keep you out of the presence of God, he will continuously bring those hurts up. A lady told me she sat in her garage in her automobile weeping about how badly her son had hurt her. "How do I get over it?" she asked. "How, how, how do I get over it? I'll go two or three days and be fine, but then I get mad and call him up or see him and say a lot of mean, ugly things. How do I get over this hurt?" I said, "Quit digging the scab off that sore. Leave it alone." If my children and I are at odds with each other, the last thing I need to do is keep digging. I watched one of our padded chairs start off with a real small needle hole in it. A month later it was the size of a button. Three months later, it was the size of a pepperoni, and now the whole back is ripped off. There was a little hurt, a little pin hole, and somebody just kept picking and tearing at it. If you allow the enemy to keep picking and tearing at your mind and your memory, soon he will make you a basket case.

Every so often, after I've typed pages and pages on my computer, I'll try to save and it won't save. A message pops up and tells me there is no room. Then I have to go back through all of the stored memory and clean out some things to make room for more.

Ask God to take some of the junk out and let the good stuff-His Word-come in and take its place. I'm learning to say, "Lord, as you show me the trash in my mind and memory, help me to get it out. Help me be man enough to deal with it, and repent of it. Then, God, by your Spirit, come in and store what needs to be stored in there."

Remember the good things of the Lord.

CHAPTER SEVENTEEN

REVERSING THE MEMORY

Remember ye not the former things, neither consider the things of old. Behold, I will do a new thing...

Isaiah 43:18-19a

I believe God uses things that are out of our control to bless us. It really doesn't matter what we think about a person, individual, or place, God is going to do what He wants to do. He uses methods that don't make sense to the world, but they stretch our faith.

Remembering the good things of God is one way to build our faith. When the enemy comes like a storm and says, "This really isn't worth it," it's so easy for the flesh to say, "You're right. It just isn't worth it." A minister friend of mine said, "When you're physically drained and mentally tired, you are open to the enemy. When your mind is weary, back off for a few days. Get out of that office and pull yourself back together. Because when you're tired and beaten, you're ripe for an attack." It's the same in marriage. We aren't tempted until we're put out with our spouse. The temptation to do wrong doesn't come when everything is great. I can look around and think, "I just had a few days off, so I'm all rested and fine and wonderful." Then I realize that those few days were six, eight, or twelve weeks ago. Other weeks I just keep saying, "One more mile. Just one more mile."

When you are tired, physically and mentally, you need to be careful. The enemy is going to find your weakest moment and then come in. When you're tired, back off, catch your breath, take a break.

When you're put out with your spouse or children, back off. Take a break. We all need a breather.

The scripture is talking about being able to forget and forgive the things that have come against us. God is saying in his word, "I'll take care of the junk." In Isaiah 41:14, we're called a bunch of little worms. When we allow things of the past to eat at us, we are nothing more than a little worm crawling around. It's time for the church to stand up and let the world see that we are more than a bunch of worms. I'm not some wiggler you put on the end of a hook to catch a bass. I'm more than that. We have more in our memory than so-and-so who hurt me in 1947 and never said he was sorry. For all these years we've remembered and can't get through to God because of it.

The Bible says to quit worrying about what's back there. Quit worrying about who hurt you. Someone told me about another church that was dedicating their new building. This person knew some people from that church had hurt me in the past and figured I'd begrudge them getting their building before we did ours. Instead I said, "Yeah, isn't it exciting. I bought some pews from them, and went back the next day and helped them landscape." You did? "Of course. I can't go through life holding a grudge. Had I let my pride stand in the way, God wouldn't have been able to bless me. Now would you rather me hold a grudge and you be sitting on the old metal chairs, or would you rather have a church full of pews for $400." I'd rather get behind me what belongs behind me, and remember the good things. If you're not careful, the enemy will make you remember-even though it was twenty years ago the boss who wronged you. He'll cause you to remember when your brother or your sister did you wrong. He doesn't want you to be together. He wants you to remember the bad things. A heartbreak that happened ten years ago can hurt just as bad today if you keep remembering it.

Once, I took sixty-five kids camping out in the Ocala National Forest. We had a hay ride, and the next morning I had them take all the hay and put it on the back of my truck-a truck I just had painted. I was going to go throw the hay out in the woods where the ranger said we could leave it. Fifteen minutes later two of the boys came back and said, "Brother Don, they wrecked your truck." I said, "I've been up all night and I've been out here for the last two days. Don't mess with me about my truck." Sure enough, a few minutes later a boy came walking back and I asked, "Where is my truck?" By now, the entire group was peeking through the bushes. For weeks, I had been preaching and teaching on forgiveness and not remembering the bad things. He said, "I cut too sharp and hit a post sticking out of the ground." He wasn't kidding. He smashed that truck from the door all the way back to the fender-and this was a club cab. Boy, I had an opportunity to show who I was. Then I had an opportunity to show who I really was. I said, "Go get my truck and come park it." All the kids were waiting, thinking, "Here's the highlight of the trip." That would have been all they remembered. Did you know that by the way you act, based on what you remember, that's all other people remember? I went back to that boy a few minutes later, just he and 1, and told him I only wanted to know one thing: "Were you hot-rodding in my truck?" He said, "No sir, I just didn't see that post." I said, "Then don't worry about it. It will be all right." That was an occasion to prove that God was God. It hurt me that he wrecked my truck: it wasn't funny. But the truck wasn't as important as influencing that entire group.

A hurt from way back when is not important enough for me to miss a blessing. The Lord said He would take all those things that come against you, all those people, all those things and rip them apart. He said He would make you brand new bright shining teeth of armor (Is. 41:15). That means He is going to put a shine on you. He'll pick you up and change your attitude. He'll show you that it's not so important to let everyone know what you know.

This One Thing I Do

Philippians 3:13 says, "But this one thing I do." In other words, if I don't do anything else, if nothing else makes a difference, there is one thing that I do. "Forgetting those things which are behind, and reaching forth." Your deliverance is not just in forgetting, you have to get on with your life. I'm going to forget what's back there and cash it out of my memory. I don't want to remember the last time she hurt me. I've already lived that hurt. I don't want her to remember the last time I hurt her. She's already had to deal with that. Now let's reach forth. We often talk about how the enemy comes against us, but we don't take time to deal with how to recover from what the enemy has done.

That verse goes on, "…reaching forth unto those things which are before," I'm going to plant seed. It's time that we reach forth and press ahead. I'm going towards my mark, I'm not going to stay back here. At a meeting one day, one of the councilmen said, "As long as we sit here and do nothing, we are cheating ourselves out of blessings from God." God can't bless unless we're reaching forth, moving ahead. We have to reach for it.

Sometime back I was looking for a way to let our community know that our church was alive, not dead. I bought flags in red, yellow, black and white and put them up outside our church, and on top of our billboard. The billboard reads "Red, yellow, black or white, you are precious in his sight." Not long after that a gentleman pulled in on a Sunday night and said, "I don't even know why I got off the interstate and came this way. But I read the sign and I turned around and read the sign again just to be sure it said what I thought it said." After the service, several of us gathered around and prayed that God would deliver him of cancer. People need to know that there is life.

Ecclesiastes 2:26a is a verse to mark in your Bible. It says, "For God giveth to a man that is good in His sight wisdom, and knowledge, and joy." Too many read this and think it means they're going to be prosperous and have a lot of money because they made things right with God. The Word hasn't even mentioned money here. It says God gives wisdom, knowledge and joy. I think we've all asked God why we have to struggle while others just snap the fingers and in comes a briefcase full of money. "Why do they have all the fancy cars? Lord, you see how they live." We have a pity party. God giveth to a man who le good in His sight, wisdom and knowledge and joy, but to the sinner He giveth travail to gather and heap up that he may give to him who le good before God. God's going to give me wisdom, knowledge and joy.

I need wisdom so I'll know how to spend what that dude who is not so good is about to give me. God uses the unrighteous to store up to give to those who are righteous in God's eyes. What I'm saying le that if someone has hurt you and you hold a grudge, God is going to send that person your way, because God believes in forgiveness. He is going to see if you're going to live and proclaim the gospel. He wants to see to it that you forgive others. He'll put them right in your face and ask, "Now what are you going to do?"

God uses the unrighteous, Sometimes, the unrighteous are greater givers than God's people. Too often, people become believers and suddenly, they have to hold on to everything. "I'm living by faith, but I can't make this commitment. But the unrighteous just spend the money. If God wanted to, he could send a suitcase full of money on the back of a cockroach. If someone comes staggering through your door and smells like a cockroach, don't run them out, they're our blessing It's the boat you've been praying for

The Smell of Service

A story is told about the pastor of the Brooklyn Tabernacle Church in New York. One Easter Sunday morning he was all decked out in fie suit, looking fine, smelling fine. After the service as he was greeting folks, he noticed a man standing halfway down the center aisle, eye balling him. The man was stinky, grungy, and nasty and as the man came towards him, the pastor thought, "Lord, all I need today is to be hit up for money by some wino." But he went and introduced himself to the man, all the while talking away from him so he didn't have to inhale the odor. That sinner recognized that the pastor didn't want to be around him. He pointed his finger at him and said, "Listen, sir, I don't want your money. I slept on your back steps last night, drunk. I woke up this morning smelly, stinking, rotten, hungry, without a home, and without a family, but I heard the music going on inside. The building was vibrating and shaking and I had to know what was going on. For the past hour, I've heard you talk about this man called Jesus. I don't want your money. I want to know about this Jesus." That pastor broke down and wrapped his arms around that smelly old sinner, realizing that was the sweetest aroma he had ever smelled in his life. From that moment, that ministry has turned around and only the Lord knows where that ministry will go and the millions of lives it will impact. All because that pastor was willing to forget that he might get hit on that morning and instead said, "I'm here to serve."

We are here to serve. We are not here to be judges. God has people out there we probably won't like, but He has preordained them to pass by our way to bless us. I heard about a Christian television station that is building a forty million dollar building. They are going to fill it with offices and rent them to the secular world. There will be enough money coming from those rental units to completely pay off the debt. God uses the unrighteous to store up to give to those that are righteous in his sight.

It is time for God's people to clear out those ugly things from the past, and let God make them from this moment afresh and anew. Then we can have the kind of faith I've been talking about. Let Him make me bright, new shiny teeth of armor. When the enemy comes against me, I want to chew him up.

I cannot reach forth as long as I'm letting something someone did to me hold me back. I want God to set us free. Pray, "Lord, I reach forth so you can use me. God, whatever you want to do in my life, I'm reaching for the things of God."

CHAPTER EIGHTEEN

THE BODY UNDER ATTACK

If the enemy can't work on your will, emotions, mind, imagination, memory or intellect, he comes against your body. We have all been I sick, and had things go wrong in our bodies that we didn't understand. I think I'm too young to have the kind of pain I have. But through study and research in the Scriptures, I am realizing two things. One, that this may be nothing more than an attack of the enemy. Two, because there are areas in my life that don't completely line up with God's Word, He can't bless me with the fruit He wants to bless me.

We have to line up with the Word. We can't take authority until we understand that we have authority. In Titus 2:15, God said that we have authority, no matter what comes against us. If that headache comes, say, "In the name of Jesus, go." People tell me they've said that, but nothing happens. But did you put the Word with it? There is a difference. You can threaten a child all you want and it won't mean nearly as much as if you bring out the old strap and say, "Now I'm going to show you what I've been trying to tell you." Sometimes we have to take the Word and say, "Devil I'm about to show you what I've been trying to tell you. You're not welcome in this body. You're not welcome in this vessel and I'm not going to give in to what you want to do to me."

The Word is alive. The Word is truth. Just as the enemy can attack the soulless parts of a human being, the human body is also a prime target. It can be as greatly hindered as the soul. The human body was given by God to show His handiwork. I'll admit I sometimes look in the mirror and say, "This doesn't look like handiwork." Do you know we cut God down when we talk about His handiwork that way? There isn't one individual in this world who looks exactly like another. Can you imagine what an imagination God must have? We shouldn't criticize God's handiwork. This body is a vessel, a tabernacle.

But the trouble is, what I am on the outside is not what I am on the inside. This flesh is going to die. The Bible says from dust it came and to dust it will go. When an astronaut goes to the moon, he wears a funny little suit to house his body. If he got to the moon and got out and walked around without the suit, his body would die. Someday my body is going to quit living and my spirit will be out of here. Doesn't it make sense that the enemy wants to come against you with a disease or a sickness? He knows what that body houses. We may look at ourselves and see broken limbs and things that don't function right, but that doesn't matter. Whether you can walk or not, whether you can hear or not doesn't matter. You have a spirit, and this old body simply houses that spirit.

In Romans 12:1, Paul says, "I beseech you therefore, brethren, by the mercies of God, that ye present your bodies a living sacrifice, holy, acceptable unto God, which is your reasonable service." It is reasonable for you to take care of this body. Let's face it, if you abuse it, you lose it. God intends for a lot of us to have an impact on this world for fifty, sixty, seventy, eighty, or ninety years. But if we don't take care of this house, this vessel, the enemy is allowed to come in and destroy it. And when the body is dead, the spirit has to go. Does that mean if God intended you to live and serve Him for ninety years, and you abused your body and had to leave here after fifty years, you won't go to heaven? We're not debating heaven or hell here. When it is your time to go, or when you make it your time to go, then you'll go for whatever rewards you've worked for.

This body is to be presented to God in a holy manner. The world cannot see spiritually. When we live like death warmed over but say we're children of God, what image are we presenting to a world that only sees in the natural? Not only does God use this body to house the spirit man, he uses this vessel to present holiness to a lost and dying world. The world looks at me to see if I am what my mouth says that I am. If I say I've been delivered from alcohol but the world sees this body hanging out in the bar, they're going to think I'm a liar.

We have a responsibility to take care of what God has given us. I can't help it that some of us are nine feet tall and some of us are three feet tall. What is important is that when I look at you, my spirit can say, "I bear witness with that spirit."

With the natural senses we taste, feel, smell and see. When we allow those senses to run havoc, they kill the spirit man. The enemy uses the senses to kill the spirit. I can be on my way to the house of God to preach the word and someone can cut me off on the highway and ruin my entire day-if I let it.

It's a job to block out what is going on around us. It's tough to get focused. When Christ's followers went to the upper room they didn't just gather and poof, they received the Holy Ghost. It wasn't easy. I don't believe they stayed in one mind and of one accord for fifteen days and then God said, "Okay, now I'm going to fulfill my word." I believe 99% were in one mind and one accord and when that other 1% finally joined them, immediately that mighty rushing wind came.

As believers, we have to get out of the flesh. I've had people tell me they can't worship because they have a headache, or because their big toe hurts. That's like saying, "I've been sitting down all day on the job and I just can't sit there for another thirty minutes and listen to God's Word." Or, "I've already had four and a half hours of Christ in my life this week, I can't take another hour."

Make Time

We cheat God out of ways to give miracles to the body of Christ.

Suppose someone comes to you with an urgent prayer request and you say, "I'll pray about it, but not right now. I don't have time." We have to make time. The Bible says, "Walk in the Spirit, and ye shall not fulfill the lust of the flesh" (Gal. 5:16). In the natural, I may be totally beat, but when I begin to talk about spiritual things, something comes alive. The Spirit takes control. The enemy comes and takes away from the Spirit because we get wrapped up in our headaches and the blister on our little toe.

Romans 12:2 goes on to say, "And be not conformed to this world: but be ye transformed by the renewing of your mind, that ye may prove what is that good, and acceptable, and perfect, will of God."

We drove up the interstate one night on our way home after sitting in meetings for two days. I'd had enough of meetings. With a body like mine, if I sit there long enough, it gets all locked up and I start seeing three of everything. I was all tense and didn't want to be messed with. Wouldn't you know, this gentleman got in the passing lane and just stayed there. The faster I'd go, the slower he would get. Every chance he could, he'd get beside a vehicle and just sit there. I just rode along until I was able to get around him. My wife looked over and said, "That was a jerk, but I'm really proud of your response. You didn't get upset, try to run him off the road, or give him a dirty look or a funny wave. You were good."

Although I didn't feel very spiritual at that moment, it was important for somebody to see me act like what I believe. If I'm wearing a tag that says Christian, I better act like it. I better tell this flesh to shut up because the world is watching. More Christians get cursed out than worldly folks, because a lot of believers say one thing but live another. Don't think because you're out on the interstate nobody knows who you are. You'd be surprised.

Suppose the gentleman who annoyed me in the passing lane had been the same one I mentioned in the last chapter, who saw our bill-board and came to our church needing prayer? Suppose I had given him a dirty look? If we're going to pray, "Lord, whoever you send our way we will minister to," we'd better get the body under control.

Since the body is so important, I don't doubt the enemy wants to come against it and put disease in it. If he can get you down in your back, you won't be able to go to the house of God. If he can get you down in your mind because your body is so full of pain, then even if you did go, you wouldn't be worth killing. The Word says when you're sick, call for someone who knows God and say, "I'm hurting and I need someone to anoint me so I can recover from this thing" (Jas. 5:14).

In 1 Corinthians 3:16 we are told, "Know ye not that ye are the temple of God, and that the Spirit of God dwelleth in you?" The next time you go out to eat, and you're going to make a glutton of yourself, turn to 1 Corinthians 3:16 and ask yourself, "Know ye not...?" If you kill the flesh, the spirit has to go and God's will not be fully worked in your life.

Know Ye Not?

Often, we live foolishly. We believe God can heal someone else, but we don't think he can heal us. A lady whose body God had healed became sick again. She came and said, "Pray for me, that I would have strength. I can't rightfully ask for a miracle." When I asked why not, she answered, "Because I already had my one miracle." God is so much bigger than that. Because of His grace and mercy and love for me, every time I fall down, He's hoping I'll ask Him to pick me up one more time.

Our body is the temple in which the Spirit of God dwells. He didn't say maybe, possibly, if you live just right, or get enough gold stars. He was emphatic with this statement. "Don't you know?" I wish Adam would have said to Eve, "Don't you know what you are about to do?" Instead, he was led, and now we have to fight off disease and sicknesses and go out and work like dogs. Women just can't bear children and say, "Praise God, wasn't this wonderful." They have to suffer pain because of the fall. The enemy came against them in the flesh.

In 1 Corinthians we read, "All things are lawful unto me, but all things are not expedient: all things are lawful for me, but I will not be brought under the power of any. Meats for the belly, and the belly for meats: but God shall destroy both it and them. Now the body is not for fornication, but for the Lord; and the Lord for the body. And God hath both raised up the Lord, and will also raise us up by His own power. Know ye not that your bodies are the members of Christ?" (6:12-15). Why does the Word keep going back and repeating itself? There is something spectacular here, but we've made light of it. We're born into the world without choice, but then we get to choose whether we want to burn in hell, or live in heaven. Too many of us live like hell, hoping we can get to heaven. We worry ourselves to death, beat ourselves to death, abuse ourselves to death, misuse ourselves to death, exhaust ourselves and won't take a day to rest to save our lives. We abuse the temple of God.

I would give anything if I could back up twenty years and listen to all the old timers who said I needed to work smarter, not harder. Some of you have something physically wrong that you know is the result of the last twenty or thirty years. If bananas hurt you, then stop eating bananas. Nothing does me more personal damage then having to sit behind a desk day after day. My body was not made to just sit there. Recently I spent several days working outside with my Dad. We worked and we worked hard. I was tired, but I felt better than I'd felt in a long time. If all you do is run and jump and holler, then sometimes you need to sit down and let that body rest. And if all you do is sit down behind a desk, sometimes you need to jump up and go mow the lawn. The Bible talks about a balanced life.

1 Corinthians 6:15 continues, "Know ye not that your bodies are the members of Christ? Shall I then take the members of Christ, and make them the members of an harlot? God forbid." Shall I take this blessed vessel and make a whoremonger out of it? God forbid! If I know that sitting behind a desk is killing this body, then God forbid that I just sit there and die.

I get after my father all the time. Recently he changed two tractor tires in two days, but he'd only worked the tractor for two hours! That's crazy! There comes a time when we have to start listening. This body houses something very important. If we kill this body, if we worry ourselves into a heart attack or until our mind leaves us, then we can't function the way God wants us to function. Once when I was so frustrated with life, my older brother said, "You have a choice. You can worry yourself to death or worry yourself crazy. But if you get good and crazy, you're not going to be a bit of good to your wife and the two children God made you responsible for. Or you can step up to the pitcher's mound and say, I'm going to throw the balls instead of the balls coming at me. I'm going to change this thing. I'm either going to worry or I'm not.

We need to listen to these old bodies, because they house a very important part of God's creation. If you live in an earthly home long enough, the roof is going to start leaking and then you have a choice. You either repair that roof so it does not destroy the substance, or you lose that house. When this old roof begins to leak, that is God's way of saying, "Hello, I didn't design that body to hurt the way it is hurting, so something is wrong." So what do we do then? Get into the Scriptures and find one that deals with what you are dealing with, and command that body to function the way you want it to function. This is hard stuff. Dying on the cross was hard. Being cursed, beaten, and spit on, was tough. But He conquered. He said if I would believe His Word, I'd not only do what He did, but even greater works shall I do (John 14:12). He wants us to do a greater work, so take care of what God has given us.

1 Corinthians 6:16 says this, "What? Know ye not that he which is joined to an harlot is one body? For two, saith he, shall be one flesh." Be careful with whom you join yourselves. If you know God blessed you and is working in your life, but there is filth going on in the workplace, be careful what you buy into. I try to tell young couples to be careful. Don't be unequally yoked together with unbelievers. It says if you join yourself with a harlot then that's what you are.

If you are a believer, you don't belong to yourself. You're not your own. You can act just as big and bad as you choose to act, but you're not your own. The only boldness you should have about yourself is the boldness in the Holy Ghost. Just like God gave part of His substance and entrusted it to you, He gave it to you so that you could give it. And if you do what is right with it, He'll give you some more.

He'll give us more than our cup can handle. He'll give you more good health than your cup can handle. Somebody has to take authority. For ye are bought with a price. The Scripture just said we're not our own, because we are bought with a price. Therefore glorify God in your body and in your spirit which are God's (1 Cor. 6:20).

When the flesh is out of control, it can dominate your spirit man. It's tough. When I went out to hang flags, I had to climb a sixty-foot flag pole. It scared me to death. That was a life challenge for me. I saw my life flash right before me. Sometimes it's scary to stand up and say, "I'm not going to hurt anymore." It's frightening to say, "I'm going to take a step. I'm going to bless Him with what He blessed me." Know that just as soon as you prove yourself in that vein, the enemy is going to come against you and say, "You fool, you gave your last dollar." My body is the temple of the Holy Ghost. When we take authority, the enemy is not going to be so quick to come against what belongs to God.

CHAPTER NINETEEN

HEALING WORDS

We have an obligation to do things differently. We need to watch different things. We need to carry on different conversations. Instead of watching "As the Stomach Turns," we W need to be into "As God Turns."

If you do what you've always done, you're going to have what you've always had. When I was a kid, my Dad would whoop me and say, "Now if you do it again, I'm going to whoop you again." When I got tired of being whooped for doing the same thing, I quit doing it. Then I got whooped for something else.

We must learn how to fight off the attacks of the enemy through the Word, instead of doing nothing. There isn't anything worse than a group of believers who will agree with the Word, but do nothing. People tell me it's not their fault if no one gets saved. Well, let's turn this thing around. The Bible says that if we will compel them, they will come in (Luke 14:23). That's how we fight off the attacks of the enemy in other people's lives, too. We go out and speak the written Word of God and compel that sinner to come in. When they get in, we don't just sit there and do nothing, we get up and do something about it. Aren't you glad somebody took you by the hand and prayed you through to salvation? Aren't you glad that when you are in need and hurting, and when things are going on in your life that you don't understand, there is a friend? That is what believers are supposed to be about. God doesn't need us to just sit there.

The Power of Words

We need to quit making it so easy for the enemy to invade our lives. We tell God we don't want cancer, but we'll do things that cause cancer. We don't want to have a bad attitude because the enemy wants us to have a bad attitude, but all we do is talk about bad things. We want to know God in a supernatural way, but don't have time to read the Word. We're just making the devil's job easy. He's just sitting back having a beach day. No sweat. Those people don't pray, don't read, and wouldn't know the Word if it slapped them upside the head. He likes believers like that.

Our words may not hurt the enemy, but when we start speaking God's Word, he can't touch that. Proverbs 18:21 tells us that, "Death and life are in the power of the tongue: and they that love it shall eat the fruit thereof." What you believe and what you speak not only affects your body, but your immune system as well. I can let pressure get to me, and before long I'm tense. After I'm tensed up, my head hurts, and after my head hurts, my nerves are shot and my conversation is dangerous. I generally feel pretty good until I get tense and then try to hold it in. My wife told me it does me more damage to hold it in than to get it out. I said, "I'm trying to be better." She said, "You're better, but you still look like a stick of dynamite that wants to go off."

Your words become either a blessing or a curse to you. When the enemy puts disease on us, we need to be healed. The Word will not only heal you, the Word will set you free. He'll set you free from the attacks of the enemy and will heal you from what the enemy has placed on your life. He will also give you a word to speak that will bring life and blessings. We have to be truthful about what's happening in our lives, but we don't have to wallow in the mud. If I go up to certain people and say I have a headache, I guarantee they'll tell me they have something worse than that.

We were at a ball game one day and a gentleman near us was hooting and hollering enough to drive me crazy. Every time I'd say, "Yeah," he'd say, "Yeah." I said, "Go get 'em Kit," and he'd say, "Go get 'em Kit." He didn't know what he was yelling. Sometimes we listen to so much garbage that it becomes a part of our lives and we don't even know what we are saying.

We have to be careful what we say. We have to be careful about accepting that headache. Let's tell the devil to take his headache and get out of our lives. We'll know he's gone when the headache is gone. People tell me they don't know when the devil is there and when he's not. Oh, you'll know, because something is not going to function the way it should. And when something's not functioning the way it should, know there is an attack coming against you. When that happens, get in the Word and speak the Word.

Proverbs 18:7 says, "A fool's mouth is his destruction, and his lips are the snare of his soul." "The tongue is a fire, a world of iniquity: so is the tongue among our members, that it defileth the whole body, and setteth on fire the course of nature; and it is set on fire of hell" (Jas. 3:6). Negative thinking in your own personal life will absolutely set the course you take. Your heart will say that truth and righteousness are this way, but the flesh will swell up and say, "There's a conversation over here that you can use to fight your cause."

Receive His Gifts

We must learn to discern what is God and what is not God. If you can't find it in the Word, it is not God. The Bible tells me I can be healed in my body. The Bible tells me I don't have to be bound by the fiery darts of the enemy. It tells me I may get thrown in the lion's den, but I can come out if I want to. I'm not going to sit around wondering who is going to throw me a rope or a ladder to get me out, I'm just going to say, "Praise God, I know I'm coming out."

When the enemy comes against us, it is important to know we can survive those attacks through God's Word. Psalms 107:20 tells us that God sent his Word and healed them. Not too long ago our church prayed for several babies. The report came back that the baby with the brain tumor is now perfect. I believe somebody put God's Word to the test and God sent His Word and healed that child.

I heard a preacher say he believed God has a warehouse full of gifts that have never been received. From top to bottom, it is packed with gifts with people's names on them-gifts they never received. They were spiritually not home when God came by to hand out their gift. If you have been seeking a miracle and wondering why you can't get a miracle, you may have had your eyes closed when Jesus came by. I told a minister friend that our people no longer expect me to call a staff or council meeting to see if we want to buy a piece of carpet for the front door. God may be standing there trying to give us something and we don't have time to ask the people if they want a miracle. We want what God will give us.

Proverbs 4:20-22 says, "My son, attend to my words; incline thine ear unto my sayings. Let them not depart from thine eyes; keep them in the midst of thine heart. For they are life unto those that find them, and health to all their flesh." God is saying, "My son, my daughter, attend, pay attention to my words. Listen to what I'm saying to you, it's not as hard as you think it is." Incline, tune in, turn off the television, quit talking for five minutes and listen to what the Spirit of God is saying.

The enemy comes to steal, kill, and destroy, but God came to bring life. He's bringing life to those who will receive, those who will do more than say, "I've heard that before." Get up and say something. Respond in some way. If your neck hurts, start doing something you've never done before. Watch God come because of His spoken Word and heal your body.

James 1:21 admonishes us to receive with meekness the engrafted Word which is able to save your souls. Have you ever seen someone carve their name on a tree or in wet concrete? They engraft it. It means we read God's Word with an open mind and heart-without being a Thomas saying, "God I've never seen this happen, but you said it happened, so I believe it. I know you are God and that you can't lie, because I read that." Perhaps Titus 1:2 should be the most important verse of our lives: "In hope of eternal life, which God, that cannot lie, promised before the world began," God said He is not a respecter of persons (Acts 10:34). If He healed me, He will heal you, because He is not a liar. He's bound to His promise, He's bound to His Word. I may not have experienced it in my life, but He has engrafted it in my spirit.

I've never seen a person's limb grow from one length to another, but my mother has. I've seen people limping one day and walking the next, but I haven't seen it happen. The Bible says to receive that engrafted Word. If you know someone with a heart condition, begin to visualize them with a new heart, because He said He doesn't use old parts. Don't you wish the car business was like the Bible? You wouldn't have to go to the junk yard for an old part that would work for a while. God reaches into His reservoir and says, "I'm just going to give a new heart. I'm going to give a new mind. I'm going to give a new limb. I'm going to take out the old nervous system and put in some new wiring."

It says to receive with meekness the engrafted Word of God because He is about to do something. When God's Spirit comes by, that which has been engrafted is going to say, "This is what I promised you. My promise is about to come alive in your life." That gives you faith to reach out like the woman with the issue of blood and take from His faith.

A pastor friend of mind began to teach his people that they were healed, delivered, set free, and blessed. He said all of a sudden his people were coming off welfare and food stamps. All of a sudden they were driving new cars and getting better jobs than the mayor has. They took the engrafted Word of God as life. They got tired of people telling them they weren't worth a flip. If you tell me that, I'll spit in your face because I don't want to hear it. I am worth something because God called me. Because of the engrafted Word of God, I know He created me and anointed me.

You fight off the attacks of the enemy when you speak the Word. Hebrews 11:3a says, "Through faith we understand that the worlds were framed by the Word of God," God spoke and poof, there is the world. How was there light? God said, "Let there be light." That tells me that without words there wouldn't be a world. God said the words He spoke, I can speak. And He said not only can you do the works that I wrought if you believe, you can do greater works (John 14:12). Jesus often healed just by speaking.

Let God and the devil know that you know and believe the Word of God. It's two-fold. When you speak God's Word, you're saying, "Father, I know your Word. I received it, I'm believing it, and I'm living it." At the same time you're saying, "Devil, no matter what you're coming against me with, greater is that Word that is in me than what you are coming against me with." Your words create images and eventually you will live out the reality of that image. I just have to listen to someone for five minutes before I have an image of what kind of person they are. Then if I skip fourteen aisles in the grocery store to stay away from them, you'll figure out what kind of image I have. A lot of folks run around calling themselves holy, but they haven't got a friend in the world. What kind of holy are they?

God's Medicine Chest

God's Word is medicine. Somebody ought to fool the devil and put the Bible in the medicine cabinet. And when he's got you on the run for another pill say, "Oops, guess what? With God's Word there isn't any overdosing and there are no side effects."

In Proverbs 4:22, God's Word is spoken of as being medicine to our flesh. It is the most powerful medicine available today and it is capable of healing your body without side effects. When attacks come against you, begin to speak from God's medicine bottle. You say, "Jesus is the Lord of my life and I forbid sin, sickness and disease to have any power over me. I am forgiven and free from sin and guilt. I am dead to sin and alive unto the righteousness of God." Begin to speak life into that situation. Colossians 1:21 says, "And you, that were sometime alienated and enemies in your mind by wicked works, yet now hath he reconciled." Wicked works are those thoughts that are contrary to God's Word. You can be your own worst nightmare by letting those wicked thoughts come. The next verse, Colossians 1:22, says, "In the body of His flesh through death, to present you holy and unblamable and unreprovable in His sight:" Jesus bore my sins in his body on a tree; therefore I am dead to sin and alive unto righteousness. I am the righteousness of God in Christ Jesus and by His stripes I am healed and made free. You can fight off the attacks of the enemy that come to your body by speaking the Word of God.

When the enemy comes against your body, you can command sickness and the enemy's attacks to go by speaking God's Word. There is a difference between knowing something and hearing about something. You can tell me you're going to punch me in the nose, and I'm going to feel one way. But when you punch me in the nose, I'm going to feel another way. Somebody needs to punch the devil in the nose. You have power. You have authority. We don't just have to say we heard God does that. We can go out there and say we know God says that.

CHAPTER TWENTY

BATTLE READY

You may be eternally secure, but as long as you live on this earth, you're going to have an enemy. People claim God wouldn't do that to us. God doesn't do that to us. But it is the way He shows us that His love, grace, mercy, power, and anointing are working in our lives so we have the power to withstand the enemy. 1 Peter 5:8 says, "Be sober, be vigilant, because your adversary the devil, as a roaring lion, walketh about, seeking whom he may devour." You're never going to be so super-spiritual that you don't have an enemy. If you are going to grow In Christ, live in Christ, and put God first, the enemy will try to mess you up.

We must know how the enemy comes against us. One of the ways is through our ignorance. We are so self-righteous. We say we don't need to read the Word, because the preacher will read it to us on Sunday. There is going to come a time in your life when you have to get in the Book and say, "God give me my revelation." I love it when a preacher encourages me; but after a while, I have to stand on my own two feet.

There is always someone watching you if you say you're a believer. I don't go from door to door saying I'm a preacher, but the whole neighborhood knows it. I have to be careful how I carry myself. You need to be careful because a temptation is going to come your way to mess up your testimony.

We have to be wise as serpents harmless as doves. We have to be wide-eyed and vigilant because we are going to be deceived if we don't look around. The enemy comes to set traps. Every person has a trap set, but God will reveal that trap to you. If we will listen to God's Spirit, He will help us overcome the attacks of the enemy.

When you allow temptation and wiles to wreak havoc in your life, it equals deception. We have all been deceived and believed in some-one who wasn't what we thought he was. We have to decide what kind of people we are going to be as believers. Are we going to go with the crowd and speak our peace, or are we going to be believers and have hearts of forgiveness? It doesn't make that wrong right, but it keeps us from being the judge.

Deception equals blindness. When you are deceived, you can't see clearly. When you allow yourself to be blinded and stay blind, it produces sin because you begin to respond to things that are contrary to God's Word.

James 3:17 says, "But the wisdom that is from above is first pure, then peaceable, gentle, and easy to be entreated, full of mercy and good fruits, without partiality, and without hypocrisy." The greatest way I know to get wisdom from above is through God's Word. It keeps me from being deceived and blinded, and turns me away from sin.

You are not fighting a person. We are not wrestling against flesh and blood, but against principalities and the rulers of the darkness (Eph. 6:12). We have to get our minds and hearts on the spiritual and say, "I'm going to walk in the Spirit and let God take care of me. He'll teach me how to pray. He'll teach me how to obey. He'll teach me what I should say."

Learn forgiveness. Let yesterday go. Get in the Word and see what it says. You can't fight off the enemy by what anyone else says. You're going to have to get a revelation and a Word for yourself.

Be Prepared

Ephesians 5:18-19 tells us, "And be not drunk with wine, wherein is excess; but be filled with the Spirit; Speaking to yourselves in psalms and hymns and spiritual songs, singing and making melody in your heart to the Lord." Turn off the country station every now and then and put God on. Do something that speaks something positive into your spirit. You've heard the old saying, "garbage in, garbage out." If you put God in, God is going to come out. You never know how much God a person has until they get in the heat of the battle.

When your spirit, soul, and body are in accord, that is a fervent prayer. God hears that because you've brought yourself under subjection and submitted yourself to the Spirit of God, saying, "God I want to hear from you. I'm going through an attack and I need your Spirit to carry me through."

The Holy Spirit is our comforter and guide. I believe God also gives us angels to take care of us. My angel knows when I'm going to do something really stupid and need protection. When somebody who is going to rub me the wrong way is coming down aisle four, I believe my angel says, "Go down aisle five," to protect me. He said He would send the comforter to help me, speak to me, love me, protect me, and keep me secure.

The devil will come at you in any way he thinks he can win. When you break one arm you are not as strong as you are with two arms. That's what happens when the body of Christ splits. You're not nearly as strong then. A family that doesn't pray together probably won't stay together. We have to be of one mind and of one accord. It would be really good if we knelt down and prayed with our family everyday, but in case that doesn't happen, we still know we are headed in the same direction. There is unity. There is also a prayer that is never spoken. It's on-going, your spirit and God's Spirit communing.

Have you ever been confused by how the enemy comes against you? One day everything was going just great, and the next your whole world had fallen apart. Confusion certainly doesn't come from God.

Samson wanted a pretty woman instead of who God had in mind for him. There are a lot of pretty things around here for us, but some-times we want somebody or something else. We can't be happy with the vehicle we drive. We make good money, but it's not enough; we have to have more. You may have to slow down and discipline yourself to learn how to live on the money you have. Because if you make a dollar and you can't make it on that, you won't be able to make it if you earn two dollars, either.

When we learn how to overcome the attacks of the enemy, God won't let us forget past victories. I don't want to relive some of the things I have had to go through, but I don't want to forget them either. Because it takes greater faith today than it did yesterday. If I look at all the things that God has helped me defeat, it's sweetness.

Heartache and Honey

In the story of Samson, we read that as he went to Timnath with his parents to get Delilah, a young lion came against him. It says Samson tore him apart with his bare hands, but he didn't tell his parents what he had done. He got Delilah, and after a while, on his way home, he saw that lion's carcass. There was a swarm of bees and that carcass was full of honey, so we know he'd been gone for a while. He scooped some of that honey out, ate it, and gave some to his parents, too (Judges 14:5-9).

I believe that lion was symbolic of the enemy and the different ways he comes against us. He can come against me through you. He can come against me through my physical condition, my will, my emotions, my intellect, my memory, my finances. There are so many different ways the enemy can come against us. Sin itself is a wild lion wanting to wreak havoc in your life.

Samson tore that lion apart because he had the power and the anointing. If you're saved, regardless of how you feel at the time, when you need God to come on the scene, God is going to be there. I don't care how scared and frantic you are, God is going to be there.

The Bible says Samson went over and dipped his hand down in the honey and picked it up. If you have ever messed with a honey hive with bees all over it with your bare hands, you got stung, right? But Samson didn't get stung. That honey is symbolic of what happens when you defeat the enemy.

If you walk with God long enough, there will come a time when the knowledge that God brought you through the battle will be like honey on your lips. It's like honey to me when I think that after lying in a bed dying of leukemia, more than thirty years later, here I stand. That builds my faith. When you've defeated the enemy, God will take you back to that place in your spirit and He'll remind you of that carcass. It represents sin that has been defeated.

When we learn how to overcome the attacks of the enemy, God won't let us forget the past victories. When God brings you back by what He's already brought you through, reach down and grab yourself a handful of honey. Come on. Reach down and say, "Give me some of that honey."

When Samson took that honey, he didn't just hoard it. Gifts are not given to keep. He took that honey and gave some to his parents. If he had told them where he got it, they would have said, "I'm not eating that stinking mess." God comes up with a handful of blessing and often, we don't want it. When God causes a carcass to spring up full of bees and honey, you are going to tell someone what God has done for you.

I spent thirty minutes talking on the telephone one day and ended up with $1,000 worth of materials delivered to our church, free and clear. That was exciting. I was anxious to tell our people about it. I wanted to share some of that honey.

Some of the things you go through may be God trying to prove to the devil that you are going to stand no matter what. Look at Job. The devil said to God, "How about Job? He's your favorite. Let me go mess with him, and see if he really loves you." God said, "You can mess with him, but you can't take his life" (Job 1:6-12). We shouldn't be so fearful. If God allows the devil to take something from you, then God has something a lot better in store for you.

A ministry grows when members who have been walking through the valley of the shadow of death start saying, "Look what God's doing. Look what God can do." I could tell that the gentleman who delivered those materials was hungry to know more about our ministry. He told me he'd noticed our flags and signs, and then he began to tell me about his 16-year-old son. I began to tell him a little bit about what God was doing in our church, and invited him to bring his family to a church cookout. I was letting that honey drip.

We get down and deceived and put out because the enemy pulled one over on us, when all the time God is just giving us a carcass to get honey out of. The honey in the carcass of that dead lion reminds us that victories are won through divine strength. We are going to have to get out of the flesh and into the Spirit. Life is a history of victory and defeat. Someday when I'm gone, I want people to say, "That was one victorious dude." What do you want people to say about you? Past victories are not to be forgotten. If you had a victory yesterday, don't forget it. Don't let super-spiritual people tell you they're tired of hearing the same old thing. Go tell someone who hasn't heard it.

If you ever have to slay a lion, be sure that eventually it will yield honey. That pain you are experiencing right now will be honey someday. I waited a long time for some past battles to be gone, and now I can honestly say I saw the spiritual gate close behind me. I don't have to live that pain anymore.

You have overcome doubt, and strengthened your faith. You have vanquished sin and increased holiness. You have conquered fear and gained strength. I don't care what the enemy tries to do to you. If you will allow God's plan to work in your life, good will come out of that evil. Somewhere out there is a carcass full of bees you are going to have to go back by. Reach down and pick up that victory God made for you. Then let God take you from there and share it with somebody. Don't hold your testimony back. If God has touched you, please go tell somebody. While you're telling your friend, somebody else is going to be listening. Let someone hear about Jesus in your life. You are a conqueror in Jesus' name.

BIBLIOGRAPHY/SOURCES USED

Nelson's New Illustrated Bible Dictionary, Copyright 1995, 1996, Thomas Nelson Publishers.

The Biblical Illustrator, by Joseph S. Exell, Copyright © 1973, Baker Book House, Grand Rapids, Michigan.

The NIV Matthew Henry Commentary In One Volume, Copyright © 1992, Zondervan Publishing House, Grand Rapids, Michigan.

Holman Bible Dictionary, Copyright © 1991, Holman Bible Publishers, Nashville, Tennessee.

The Thompson Chain Reference Bible, Copyright © 1988, B.B. Kirkbride Bible Company, Inc., Indianapolis, Indiana.

ABOUT THE AUTHOR

Don R Vining is a dedicated minister and seasoned entrepreneur, bringing over forty-five years of experience to both ministry and business. Throughout his life, Don has played a key role in planting new churches, passionately advancing the Kingdom of God through leadership, mentorship, and faithful service.

Don completed the Ministerial Internship Program under the recommendation of the State Board of Education of the Church of God. He holds ministerial credentials as an Exhorter, Licensed Minister, and Ordained Bishop with the Church of God, headquartered in Cleveland, Tennessee. In 2017, he was recognized for twenty-five years of service as a credentialed minister.

In 2002, Don was awarded an Honorary Doctor of Ministry degree from Jacksonville Theological Seminary, a recognition of his lifelong commitment to spiritual growth, leadership, and the equipping of the saints.

A devoted husband and father, Don resides in Belleview, Florida. His life and ministry are marked by a deep passion for Christ and a sincere desire to help others grow in faith through the power of spiritual understanding and transformation. His journey reflects a calling to serve, to teach, and to walk alongside others as they discover God's purpose for their lives.